NEW
LANDSCAPING
IDEAS THAT WORK

NEW
LANDSCAPING
IDEAS THAT WORK

JULIE MOIR MESSERVY

The Taunton Press

The Taunton Press
Inspiration for hands-on living®

The Taunton Press, Inc.
63 South Main Street, PO Box 5506
Newtown, CT 06470-5506
e-mail: tp@taunton.com

Editor: Peter Chapman
Copy editor: Valerie Cimino
Indexer: Barbara Mortenson
Interior design: Carol Petro
Layout: Bethany Gracia
Illustrator: Bethany Gracia
Cover photographers: front cover photos: (bottom and top left) © Mark Lohman;
(top center, right, and far right) © Susan Teare;
back cover photos: (clockwise) © Susan Teare, © Susan Teare, © Allan Mandell,
© Mark Lohman, © Lee Anne White, © Ken Gutmaker

The following names/manufacturers appearing in *New Landscaping Ideas That Work*
are trademarks: GreenThemes®, Home Outside®

Library of Congress Cataloging-in-Publication Data

Names: Messervy, Julie Moir, author.
Title: New landscaping ideas that work / author: Julie Moir Messervy.
Description: Revised edition. | Newtown, CT : Taunton Press, Inc., [2018] |
   Includes index.
Identifiers: LCCN 2017044462 | ISBN 9781631868504
Subjects: LCSH: Landscape design. | Landscape gardening.
Classification: LCC SB473 .M4462 2018 | DDC 712--dc23
LC record available at https://lccn.loc.gov/2017044462

Printed in the United States of America
10 9 8 7 6 5 4 3 2 1

ACKNOWLEDGMENTS

For this second edition of Taunton Press's popular *Landscaping Ideas That Work*, my team and I reworked much of the text and present new images and ideas to inspire and inform homeowners. In this version, we use our app to illustrate the landscape plans. The result is an updated overview of how to use the different elements that go into making landscapes that work. We hope you enjoy it.

We are so glad to be working with Executive Editor Peter Chapman and Book Art Director Rosalind Loeb once again. We appreciate their flexibility in trusting JMMDS with so many of the tasks that go into creating an elegant book. Special thanks go to photographers Tria Giovan, Ken Gutmaker, Mark Lohman, Allan Mandell, Randy O'Rourke, Susan Teare, Brian Vanden Brink, and Lee Anne White.

We could not have created this book without the talented landscape professionals who answered our call for submissions and took the time to send us such wonderful projects and the homeowners who generously allowed their properties to be photographed. I especially appreciate the contributions of Elizabeth Halley, Claire Jones, Maggie Judycki, Cynthia Knauf, Brooks Kolb, M J McCabe, Lisa Port, and John Szczepaniak. Please refer to the back of the book for more specific credits.

This book was a delight to write because of JMMDS's talented staff—there's just nothing that they cannot take on. The digital age was made for us—we are located in rural Vermont, so we need to be nimble and creative and find new ways to bring the work to us via the Internet. Bethany Gracia, our wonderful landscape and graphic designer, laid out the book with her always elegant hand and created the illustrations using our Home Outside® app; Jennifer Silver ably helped write and direct the details into place; landscape architect Erica Bowman helped write the plant chapter; and Jana Bryan and Samantha Anderson read through the final manuscript, improving and perfecting it. Please check out our landscape design app and online design service at www.homeoutside.com. And for more of our designs, books, lectures, and even a little philosophy, go to www.jmmds.com. We'd love to hear from you!

—Julie Moir Messervy

CONTENTS

INTRODUCTION

In this, the age of screens, our need for time and space in the out-of-doors is essential to our physical, mental, and even spiritual health. One way to engage with nature is to create a landscape around your house that draws you and your loved ones outside. If you build it, they will come—to bask with a cup of coffee in the early morning rays, to play hopscotch on the driveway, to harvest the ripest tomato along with a snip of basil for a fresh caprese salad, to plant a rose bush, or to catch fireflies in the grassy meadow under the stars. These real-life experiences bring to children, and adults alike, a deep connection to our earth and a rekindling of spirit that can't happen any other way.

The good news is that it's not that hard to create a landscape that works. In these pages, I walk you through the process as we do it at JMMDS, my landscape architecture and design firm, from documenting your site and figuring out your aesthetic preferences to thinking about your property from big picture all the way down to the details. We were keen to revise this book specifically because of the continued interest in landscaping and creating outdoor living spaces. There are three key reasons for this strong interest: First, both landscape improvements and outdoor living spaces continue to add value to homes, helping to make them more marketable. Second, with the improving economy, families have more available resources to upgrade their homes, and increasingly they want comfortable outdoor spaces in which to relax. And third, there is a trend toward smaller houses, especially among Baby Boomers and Millennials, so that homeowners strive to make the most of the space they do have by expanding their living space outdoors.

This new edition includes up-to-date case studies along with current photos, technical information, sidebars, and captions that feature popular residential outdoor design elements such as fire pits, outdoor kitchens, decks, and pergolas. We've included more information about low-water designs and responsible stormwater management, as well as the use of native plants that benefit insects and birds. Everyone wants comfortable living spaces in the out-of-doors, and we—and the other design professionals featured in this book—know how to help. We feature a range of projects, from luxurious spaces to those that were built with sweat equity on a shoestring. What's common to all is the quality of their designs. Be inspired!

DESIGNING

We all want a landscape that works well with

our particular site, dreams, and way of life.

YOUR

With just a little planning, your home outside

is within reach.

LANDSCAPE

Get Started

As the proud owner of a piece of property, you may feel pretty comfortable choosing paint colors for the walls and carpeting for the floors, but when you walk outside, you freeze. Without four walls, a floor, and a ceiling, you haven't the first idea of where to begin.

It can be both daunting and discouraging to try to figure out how to make landscape improvements to your property without the help of a professional designer. If you've bought a new home, the contractors probably left you with a completed house on an unfinished site; if you own an older landscape, you have to deal with someone else's taste. How do you figure out what to do? How do you even begin?

You break it down into parts. Start by understanding your property, including issues of location, sun and shade, soils, slope, and planting zone. Then look closely at your house—its size, style, layout, and inside/outside relationship. Next, think about yourself and your family—your style, your temperament, and your list of needs for your property. What do you want to have happen there?

Every site is different and each person is unique. This means that you need to do some research to better understand your property and a bit of soul-searching to figure out your particular personality, background, style, and needs. Let's get started.

top right · Many of us have no idea how to begin to create a landscape that works. This large lawn is enlivened by a swing, but it is ripe for a new, more personal design.

bottom right · You can take cues from your house's materials and style. A vertical trellis adds a feeling of enclosure to the front door of this charming cottage.

There's nothing better than living comfortably in the out-of-doors. Here, clematis vines twine up openwork lattice to bring colorful blooms to this garden room.

YOUR PROPERTY

Where you dwell—in the country, the city, or the suburbs—can affect the way you are able to live on your land. In the city, you would be very lucky to have outdoor space of your own, whether it's a roof deck, a garden, or a balcony. Instead, you may rely upon public open space like parks or community gardens to act as substitutes for your own backyard. Houses in suburban neighborhoods are often built around the needs of families, complete with private backyard spaces, driveways, and garages, with easy walking access to community amenities. Country properties might be larger in scale, with vast vistas and views, or set in a village where homes are nestled near a market, a school, and a church. In every case, your land is a precious commodity, so understanding its opportunities and constraints is critical to designing the landscape around your house.

Whether you live on a level piece of land or one that slopes will influence what you can do there. Land that slopes away from your house is desirable because it drains water away and enables long views out. Land that slopes toward your house can bring drainage headaches—a good perimeter drain helps—but enables you to look right into the upward-facing slope. When thoughtfully planted, a hillside view that can be readily seen from inside the house can almost literally bring the outside in, no matter the weather.

Once you have a good plan to work from (see "App Site Plans" on the facing page), you can start to notate the site conditions like sun and shade, topography, soils, drainage, and wind. The amount of sun and shade your property receives throughout the day and over the course of a year affects where you choose to build a patio, locate a shade tree, or situate a sunny cutting garden. In the northern hemisphere, western sun in late afternoons in

above • Increasingly, Americans are moving away from thirsty, high-maintenance turf lawns. This wildflower meadow is a beautiful, wildlife-friendly alternative.

above • In order to take advantage of every square inch, the owner of this modest home enclosed the front yard and turned it into a garden.

App Site Plans

An accurate base plan is the first step to designing your landscape, whether you're making changes to an existing design or giving your property an entire makeover. You can map out your property with pencil and paper, but it's not like drawing your living room—measuring and documenting an outdoor space can be tricky. We created our Home Outside app to help homeowners create property base plans in an easy, fun way. Follow the steps below to create your own base plan that you can use over and over to try out new design ideas and share with others.

- Open the app on your mobile device, laptop, or desktop computer and follow the tutorial instructions for importing a satellite map image of your property. Or, if you have a survey or plot plan, you can take a photo or scan and import it into the app.

- Using the Layers feature, set your map image or property plan as a separate layer and lock it so that you can't inadvertently make changes to the image.

- The app offers over 700 hand-drawn elements you can use to represent almost everything you could have or want in your home landscape. Add layers and insert structures, paths, water features, planting beds, driveways, trees, and more to indicate the locations of those elements on your property.

- Use the Sketch tool to add further detail, if you'd like. The Notes tool lets you make note of what you'd like to preserve or alter, record details, add plant names, and so on.

- Save the design as "Base Plan." Then, every time you want to try out a new idea or mock up a fresh design, you can duplicate the design, save it with a different name, and start moving the elements around, subtracting and adding whatever you'd like. It's that easy!

Start a new design using the Home Outside app and open the Map Tool.

Find your location and mark your property boundaries.

Apply the satellite image to your design, rotate, and resize to fit. Lock the layer.

Design your landscape.

summer is particularly hot and harsh, so siting a large shade tree to filter western light makes sense.

Take soil samples to learn about your soil's composition—the health of your garden's plants depends on it. Knowing the type of soil you have can help you make good choices about plant selection—not all plants can live in wet soil, for instance—but also about how to improve it. Take samples to your local extension service for analysis. As you do so, learn the hardiness zone where you live to enable you to select appropriate plantings that will thrive on your property.

Wind is yet another factor to consider as you get to know your land. By siting trees, buildings, or fences in the right spots, you can help impede the force of strong prevailing winds in your area. Similarly, make sure not to block beneficial summer breezes as you plan where to locate trees.

top right · **This narrow backyard sits up against a steep slope. We turned it into an outdoor living and dining space complete with terrace, a water feature, a play area, and beautiful plantings.**

bottom right · **This house and its landscape enjoy views to the water. The small terrace nestles against the house on level ground, while the lawn slopes steeply down the hill.**

facing page · **When a house looks into a hillside, it's fun to turn it into a garden. Here, a small pond and plantings are natural complements to the trellised open-air room.**

Foreground, Middle Ground, Background

The house where I live sits up on a hill overlooking two ponds—a circular swimming pond and a beaver pond beyond. The first thing we did was to create some level ground behind the house by building a curved retaining wall that echoes the roundness of the pond. Above the wall, we built a semicircular terrace around a fire pit, with planting beds of shrubs and perennials that form a crescent shape above the wall. Then we laid out deep planting beds against the garage, around our hot tub, and a nearby vegetable garden with curved beds that step up the south-facing hillside.

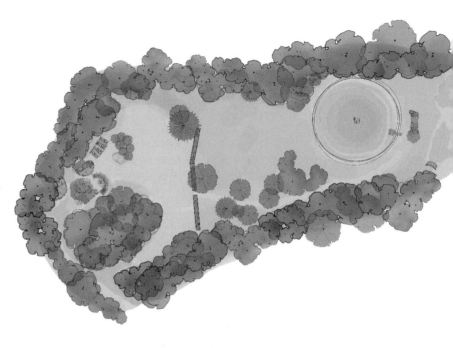

Deep planting beds act like bumpers for the grass path that leads you down the hill toward the swimming pond.

above • Our stone fire pit terrace provides a level surface for Adirondack chairs that look down onto the view of the ponds.

right • Solar panels sit neatly on the garage roof, facing south, while the level lawn offers opportunities for play.

YOUR HOUSE

When designing a landscape, take your cues from your house and its style. If you live in a Cape Cod–style cottage, for instance, you might choose to stay in the vernacular by selecting a white picket fence, whitewashed window boxes, and hydrangea plantings, along with brick or stone walkways and terraces. If you live in a more contemporary house with flat roofs and concrete and glass walls, you may prefer a clean, spare landscape of ornamental grasses, concrete walkways, and glass railings to match the architecture.

As we'll discuss in Chapters 4 and 5, your house also provides many clues as to how best to lay out paths, patios, enclosures, and special features on your land. A formal Georgian house looks great with straight lines and symmetrical planting beds, whereas a Japanese-style home is set off beautifully by asymmetric plantings, offset paths, and low-slung walls.

top right · A long sloping roof is punctuated with penetrations that let the light into the deep overhang above a garden space.

bottom right · Tall black planters stand up to the strong lines of this facade. The framed rectangles of the walkway pavers are also appropriately scaled to the entry porch; imagine a shorter rectangle at the base of the stairs, and you'll see why it works best generously sized.

This blue wall with its square windows contrasts nicely with the planting beds around it. Yellow yarrow and red cardinal flower provide a punch of color alongside the tawny-hued path.

WHAT'S YOUR STYLE?

In order to figure out what particular design style and aesthetic appeal to you, you'll need to ask yourself some questions. Are you a practical person who thinks first about the details necessary to make something work or someone who imagines first and gets the facts later? Do you hope to share your landscape with lots of people or maintain it for your own mostly private pleasure? Do you prefer an orderly landscape with everything in its place or are you happier with a relaxed and casual garden?

Similarly, ask yourself and your loved ones about aesthetic preferences. Do you like a landscape that is formal or informal? Do you prefer straight lines or curved ones? A spare, open landscape or one that's filled with plantings? Representational or abstract sculpture? Dark spaces or light ones? Uncovering everyone's preferences is helpful as you work through any design or planning process and will help you organize your wish list of projects.

top right • The layout and details of this contemporary house work well with the Japanese flavor of its courtyard garden.

bottom right • An ornate iron fence melds perfectly with the historic house and grounds that it encloses.

An Urban Terrace

This tiny front yard in Brooklyn was in need of an update. Working closely with the homeowner and her family, we laid out a new design using our Home Outside design service, without stepping foot on the property, and then detailed the large concrete stepping stones and soft woodland plantings. Now the family has a handsome entry garden that is also a relaxing little piece of nature in the city.

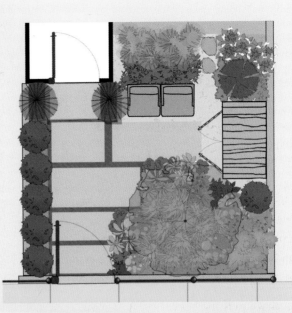

below • The overscale concrete pavers act as front path and terrace, where bright blue stadium seating offers a place to enjoy the sun and the world passing by. Plantings flourish in the garden space that softens the iron fence.

Create a Wish List

What do you and your loved ones want to actually do on your property? Do you need recreation space for young children? Multifunctioning areas for family dinners? A fire pit? A vegetable garden? A cozy corner for stringing up a hammock?

To understand better how you actually want to use your property, fill out the worksheet on the facing page. It will give you a good sense of the atmosphere you're trying to create, the activities you want to undertake, and the features that will enhance your life in the out-of-doors. Creating a wish list of desired projects helps you envision what you hope to achieve on your land in the long term and can help you make choices about phasing the projects over time.

You can also create a scrapbook or Pinterest board of ideas and images that speak to you. Find pictures of elements you want to add to your landscape and identify what style best suits your taste and temperament.

When you add up all the information about you and your family's lifestyle and needs, together with the conditions on your site and the style of your house, you get a pretty complete picture of what you can create on your land. Next is the hard part—pulling it all together into a layout that works.

top right · This homeowner longed for a colorful perennial border full of old-fashioned plants: delphinium, hollyhock, lilies, and hydrangeas.

bottom right · Many of us yearn for a more formal landscape that looks trim and neat, like this one. Clipped yew hedges lead the eye to a central fountain and the view to the water beyond.

Using Your Home Outside

How would you like to use your outdoor space? Defining the activities you'd like to engage in on your property will help define the design.

ATMOSPHERE

- ☐ *Hideaway*
- ☐ *Welcoming*
- ☐ *Relaxation*
- ☐ *Privacy*
- ☐ *Contemplation*
- ☐ *Working landscape*
- ☐ *Wildlife habitat*
- ☐ *Party central*
- ☐ _____
- ☐ _____
- ☐ _____
- ☐ _____
- ☐ _____
- ☐ _____
- ☐ _____
- ☐ _____

ACTIVITIES

- ☐ *Festive gatherings*
- ☐ *Grilling/cooking*
- ☐ *Dining*
- ☐ *Yoga/exercise*
- ☐ *Lawn games*
- ☐ *Children's play*
- ☐ *Sunbathing/stargazing*
- ☐ *Birdwatching*
- ☐ *Homesteading*
- ☐ *Gardening*
- ☐ *Animal keeping*
- ☐ *Projector movies*
- ☐ _____
- ☐ _____
- ☐ _____
- ☐ _____
- ☐ _____

FEATURES

- ☐ *Hammock*
- ☐ *Swimming pool*
- ☐ *Fire pit/fireplace*
- ☐ *Hot tub*
- ☐ *Sauna*
- ☐ *Flower garden*
- ☐ *Chicken coop*
- ☐ *Vegetable garden*
- ☐ *Reading nook*
- ☐ *Potting shed*
- ☐ *Orchard*
- ☐ *Furniture*
- ☐ *Water feature*
- ☐ _____
- ☐ _____
- ☐ _____
- ☐ _____

SPACES

Breaking your property into zones

helps define the way you live on your land.

THAT WORK

Making Space

Your property, like your house, is composed of a series of spaces with different functions. Understanding the purpose and possibilities for each of these zones on your property helps you break down the design of your landscape so that it's not quite so overwhelming.

Like your front hall or foyer, the front yard acts as a welcoming zone and entry area into the property. Similar to your living room, den, or dining room, the backyard creates wonderful opportunities for family gatherings, play, and getaways. And like a corridor or hallway in your house, a side yard offers an attractive passage that links spaces together.

Depending upon the amount of light and the topography of each, these spaces can look and feel quite different from one another. A sunny front yard will feature a very different planting palette from a shady side garden; a backyard that nestles into a planted hillside will feel far more private than a grassy front lawn that opens onto the street. As always, your own aesthetic preferences should influence how each space works and feels.

top right · **Privacy is valued both inside and out. An iron arch covered with vines creates a doorway into an outdoor room.**

bottom right · **House and landscape are united when the white stucco walls are echoed in the concrete driveway, pavers, and silvery plantings.**

Which do you prefer? Curvy, linear, or geometric? These basic layouts are good starting points for making spaces that work.

CURVY

Includes spaces that are composed of curving, rather than straight, lines. Soft arcing shapes, circles, ovals, and S-curves are appealing perhaps because they echo what we see in nature.

GEOMETRIC

Takes its cues from the built environment. Geometric incorporates shapes such as squares, rectangles, and even triangles. Replicating a shape or element of our house offers a satisfying way to link inside and outside.

LINEAR

Uses straight lines to organize the spaces around your house, making a dynamic interrelationship between structure and landscape. Pergolas, paths, patios, and enclosures can be placed parallel, perpendicular, or diagonal to the plane of your house, creating energetic alignments.

Front Yards

As properties shrink in size and space is at a premium, front yards are taking on new roles to better support the life of the family. Rather than the typical broad swath of front lawn, the front yard has become a welcoming entryway as well as a comfortable living space. No longer just made up of overgrown foundation plantings, now rain gardens, edible landscapes, and riotous perennial borders are planted in this valuable land at the front of the house.

The layout of your front yard also conveys the first impression visitors have of your home, and, by extension, your personality. A lively, colorful cottage garden centered on a painted bench gives passersby a very different image of who you are than would a bland open lawn.

There are special problems and opportunities that affect the design of a front yard. When the house sits far above or below the street, getting to it requires thoughtful planning. Similarly, if a house rests too close to a street, it pays to enclose the front yard, not only for safety's sake, but to increase usability as well. Reframe your thinking: What if you treated your front yard as though it were a backyard? How would it function differently from the way it does right now?

top right • Placing large objects into a small space can make it feel much bigger than it actually is. These broad concrete pavers serve as a terrace for someone sitting on the stadium seating—a basking place in this front-yard oasis in the city.

bottom right • This suburban home could have featured a large sweep of lawn, but the homeowners decided to plant it with drought-tolerant shrubs and perennials and a river stone path running from the sidewalk to the backyard.

right • The clean lines of this house are well matched by the planting beds of liriope, the square raised planter boxes, and the trimmed hedges below the windows.

below • This front porch welcomes all visitors by inviting them up onto a stone patio. The combination of gateways of finials and clay pots, together with the stepping stone set into the walkway, beckons us inward.

A Family Play Yard

When you live in a suburb not far from a teeming metropolis, you learn to value every piece of usable ground. In this neighborhood, the narrow front yard faces south and has been turned into a soccer field and play space for a family with young children. To do this, we removed old sprawling hedges and installed narrower varieties instead, giving maximum width for play. Above the lawn, new retaining walls, complete with planters, create a beautiful usable terrace facing the street.

A side yard also expands the space to include wide steps that double as outdoor seating and a long bluestone entertainment terrace that terminates in an exedra bench and gas fire pit. Beyond the terrace, tall trees and shrub plantings create a lush backdrop and bring shelter and privacy.

above • This home outside is a mecca of active play that attracts the whole neighborhood.

left • A bluestone terrace along the front of the house helps create usable space but also adds depth to the flat facade of the house, all softened by beautiful plantings.

facing page top • The U-shaped stone bench enables a crowd of young people to enjoy the square fire pit, which is especially magical at night.

facing page bottom right • The fire pit's bluestone cap is wide enough to use as a table, a resting space for s'mores, or an outdoor footstool. Moveable furniture adds flexibility and creates a conversation area around the focal fire element.

STEPPED FRONT YARDS

Not everyone lives on level ground. Sloping front yards and houses that sit high above (or below) the street require a series of stairs or steps to reach the front door. With thoughtful design, the experience of scaling a height can be exciting and rewarding, rather than arduous.

Think of a series of steps and landings like a waterfall. The front door is the "origin" of the falls; the front stoop or porch is where it "dams up" and then flows down the steps, pooling where landings occur, until it "spills" out to meet the road or sidewalk below.

Make the steps wide enough for two people to walk side by side, complete with landings every few feet of rise so that visitors can catch their breath. For safety's sake, place lights so that every step is well lit. Direct water runoff into adjacent planting beds or lawn areas so that the steps remain dry.

above · Working with the adjacent retaining wall and planting beds, this staircase defines a threshold between public and private space (the sidewalk and the front yard). The threshold is strengthened by the use of symmetrical shrub plantings on either side of the staircase.

left · Landscape steps look and feel good when the riser is low and the tread is long and deep. Here, a long level deck that sits one step up from the walkway leads visitors to the front door.

facing page · New stone walls, lights, railings, steps, and path marry well with the existing stone retaining wall. Notice how the walkway widens out to become the landing for the ever-narrowing steps.

ENCLOSED FRONT YARDS

When you place a wall, fence, or hedge around your front yard, you turn it into something special. An enclosed space along the sidewalk provides a protected place for sitting as well as an edge against which you can plant your favorite flowers. Your front yard becomes your front garden and shows off a bit of your personal style to the world.

Surrounding the front of your property with low hedges or fencing helps keep the world out and children in, while still allowing passersby to look in and enjoy what they see. Such front yards present a useful alternative to traditional lawn-and-foundation planting designs, especially where space is at a premium. Why not use the front of your house for living, entertaining, and play, just as you do the backyard, and make the most of the real estate?

above · This front yard sits right on the street, protected by a handsome wooden fence with an openwork topper and softened by grasses and plantings. We all wish we could look inside!

left · This courtyard is taken up by a large ornamental pool and fountain, cooling the air and offering trickling sounds for those lucky souls who live there.

A Gated Garden

A narrow picket fence is punctuated by a tall wooden structure that frames views to a beautiful garden beyond. The low, hinged gates are thoughtfully detailed to carry the pickets through a frame that can either block or enable access from the lane. Once inside, a visitor meanders along a peastone path, edged with pruned boxwood and other bushes.

right · **The slightly open gate beckons us to enter and begin an enticing journey through the garden.**

below · **Peastone walkways contrast beautifully with the clipped hedges and widen into spaces large enough to accommodate seating. A stone walkway to the front door cuts right through.**

Side Yards

Depending upon your property, a side yard can be a narrow sliver of space between buildings or an area wide enough to house a garage or even a terrace. In either case, a side yard can feel oddly separate from the rest of the property if its design doesn't include details—like plantings or hardscape features that are repeated in the front yard or backyard—that integrate the side yard into the entire design.

What unites most side yards is their function as passageway between front yard and backyard. It is important to design a path that flows easily between spaces. Do you want a functional walkway that serves as the shortest distance between two often-visited points? Or would you like a meandering stepping-stone path that slows you down enough to notice a lovely plant, an attractive framed view, or an interesting focal point?

Hemmed in by buildings as these spaces can be, light and air circulation often require consideration. The use of open styles of fencing, where fencing is needed, can permit more light and a greater sense of spaciousness. Many utilitarian items can be housed in a side yard, such as a tool shed, compost bin, dog run, or grill, because this space is often just out of public view.

In planning your side yard, don't forget the neighbors. If privacy is a concern, erect a high fence or tall

top right • Massive round stepping stones link the front yard to a narrow side garden. Bamboo culms erupt along the wall and make the long straight path to the back more inviting.

bottom right • Side yards often double as closets or storage areas. Here, firewood is stacked high and cleanly along a stone pathway.

facing page • Sometimes a side yard just wants to be a garden. Although narrow, this verdant, shady space is sized just for one—a contemplative nook along the way.

A random rectangular walkway leads visitors a goodly distance from driveway to front door, curving softly amongst plantings and around the facade in this handsome side yard.

plantings to block visual and physical access between yards. By adding a gate, you can keep the relationship between the properties strong.

Similar to a front yard, a roomy side yard can also function the way a backyard does: for entertaining, dining, or relaxation. And if your kitchen door opens onto your side yard, it's also a wonderful place to locate a grill or pizza oven. Just make sure to include a buffet table and some comfortable chairs nearby, so the grillmeister of the family can socialize while serving up the meal.

left • A black metal gate allows visual access while controlling who can enter and leave. Along the way, a beautiful garden of billowing shrubs and perennials makes the long concrete paver walkway feel more relaxed.

below • Tomatoes and other edibles find sun along this south-facing shallow side yard. Narrow wooden sheds double as a fence along the street side.

Backyards

When we want to get outside, we usually gravitate to the backyard, where all manner of outdoor living can occur. Behind our house, protected from passersby or neighbors' view, we feel the freedom to do—and be—whatever we want. The best backyards enjoy a comfortable relationship between inside and outside, visual screening from neighbors for privacy, and an interesting view or focal point, either on the property itself or beyond its bounds.

Whereas a front yard creates the first impression visitors will have of your home and should make you and your guests feel welcomed, the backyard exists to lure people outside. It should look inviting from indoors, and it could serve any number of functions (and often several at once). Your backyard might be a space for entertaining and family dining, recreation and children's play, relaxing and having quiet time, hobbies such as gardening or painting, and just spending time outdoors (for all household members—human and otherwise). Even the tiniest backyard, thoughtfully designed, can accommodate most if not all of these needs for gathering, for play, and for getting away.

Unless you're lucky enough to have a large property with grand vistas, you probably will want to enclose your backyard with a fence, hedge, or wall high enough to keep prying eyes out and children (and dogs) in. At the same time, adding large windows and French doors to the back of your house encourages easy visual and physical access between inside and out.

top right · Swinging benches remind us of the reason backyards exist—to kick back and relax on your own or with a loved one.

bottom right · Fire pits bring a bit of the campground to our own backyards. This one is surrounded by plantings and made private by a high wooden fence along the property line—it's a place we want to be.

This backyard has just about everything we'd ever want in one small place: privacy, comfortable seating around a big dining table, an interesting water feature, and plantings galore.

GATHERING SPACES

Most of us long to turn our backyard into a place where family and friends love to gather, whether it be for dining out under the stars or sitting around the fire pit making s'mores and conversation. All you need is a level area–paved or decked is best— that allows safe and easy passage between house and landscape and extends the floor of your house outside. Easy access to your kitchen always helps.

right • This backyard terrace garden is enlivened by royal purple seat cushions that complement the chartreuse-painted metal chairs and table.

A huge window wall marries inside to outside, where gathering happens at a large scale.

A few steps down and you're nestled on an outdoor sectional right next to a stone fire pit complete with protective back, making this gathering space a true outdoor living room.

left · A peastone terrace is a good-looking, lower-cost alternative to stone pavers and is well suited to the informal beauty of this rustic setting. The stone edging keeps the pebbles from tumbling down into the lawn.

This house is nearly dwarfed by the large terrace
that takes pleasure in gathering people together.
The eclectic mix of furniture styles and uses
breaks the space up into rooms.

Getaway and Gathering Spaces

Those of us who have small properties may not feel that we can create both gathering and getaway areas in our limited backyards. But here, just steps from each other, Robert Hanss designed just that: A bluestone terrace holds a dining table and chairs, separated by ground-cover plantings and trees from a wooden platform deck designed just for two that is nestled into the corner.

right · It helps to have greenery around the contemplative sitting area. An interesting water feature, along with the stepping-stone slabs, links the two.

below · In this small backyard, two distinct areas made of different materials for different purposes are linked together by a long horizontal wooden-slatted fence that gives complete privacy from the neighboring yard.

GETAWAYS

Your backyard landscape is not only ideal for gathering; it also can provide the perfect spot for getting away. Finding a cozy corner to hang a hammock, place a bench, or set out a chaise longue creates a place to stop all activity and just kick back and relax. Even better, locate your getaway where you're shaded beneath a leafy bough or nestled up against a perimeter wall or high fence, or find a spot for an arbor or pergola sized just for an intimate two. Even in the tiniest yard, finding the spot that feels somewhat remote yet not too far from the action creates a delightful adult daydreaming place— one we all deserve.

above • Climb three circular steps to the very top and you'll find a lacy metal chair that nestles against a fieldstone wall, backed up by voluptuous plantings.

Who says you can't create a private retreat on a busy street? Just place it behind a thick planting of trees and shrubs and nestle right in.

Overhead structures like this wisteria-clad corncrib feel like a secret room on a large property like this one. Note the candelabra that lights up the structure at night.

PLAY SPACES

Now more than ever, our backyard landscapes need to draw kids outside so they get away from computer and television screens and into nature once more. The many benefits of outdoor play include being active, collaborative, and imaginative. It doesn't take much to delight children.

Play spaces can be simple or elaborate, depending on budget, imagination, and inclination. You may choose to create a fairy-tale tree house, tempting hobbit hole, or perfect sandbox . . . but if you don't, children will create their own play from a low-hanging tree branch, the crawl space under some overgrown shrubs, or a small muddy spot behind the garage. Just as old-time gardeners used to leave an untended corner for the fairies, make sure to leave a place in your yard for imaginative play. And remember that play is not just for children, either!

below • A swing set need not take up your whole yard. Here a snag is ingeniously repurposed as a support for children's swings. A neat bed of bark mulch provides cushioning while preventing the unsightly under-swing dead-grass effect.

above • Some play equipment can be integrated right into your garden beds. These square planks create a challenging balance beam set close to the soft mulched ground and a safe stone for perching.

above • What child doesn't long to ride on a horse, in their own backyard? This tire swing gets pretty close.

A backyard bocce court doubles as an attractive garden, complete with sculpture inspired by the game.

Driveways and Garages

Driveways and garages—among the most utilitarian of landscape features—are not necessarily the most attractive, but thoughtful design can make them downright beautiful as well as useful.

If you are starting from scratch and can choose where to situate a driveway or garage, weigh the options very carefully—you will live with these choices every day. Where possible, locating the garage close to the kitchen of your house makes it easy to move kids, groceries, and trash between buildings. If the garage is unattached, building a roofed connection between garage and house keeps the path between the two dry and safe, especially in winter. Consider the shape of your driveway—a curved drive in front of the house can make the most of an underused front lawn, or a straight shot down the side of the property can be tucked out of the way, with access to side and back doors.

If you don't have the luxury of selecting the location of your driveway and garage, make the best of the existing plan by using plants to soften their appearance and make them part of the landscape. Add paths wherever needed to enhance ease of access. The appearance of a garage can be altered with paint, different roofing material, or "jewelry" such as light fixtures to better match your house and landscape.

Driveways can be of many varied materials. Look for water-permeable options that reduce storm-water runoff; these can be among the most affordable paving options and include grass, gravel, stone, recycled plastic grid systems, permeable asphalt, pervious concrete, or good old-fashioned paving strips (see "Making Tracks," p. 52).

above • The clean, flat roof and wide opening of the attached garage work nicely with the attractive terracelike paving pattern of the driveway.

above • A garage can double as a guest house or apartment under the eaves. This one is made more appealing by the addition of a trellis covered with wisteria vines.

right • The front of this unattached garage houses a car; the back was turned into a tool shed, all reached by stone tire tracks that double as a garden path.

below • This peastone driveway, edged with cobbles at the street, looks more like a garden than a space for cars, thanks to the plantings and the tree that breaks up the space.

A Shared Driveway

Sharing a driveway doesn't have to mean giving up your privacy. This residence in Falls Church, Virginia, is one of two homes built on a former single home lot—now 6,000 square feet each. A communal driveway bisects the two properties and leads to two garages at the back. Landscape designer Maggie Judycki of GreenThemes® used walls, fences, decking, and walkways to create a handsome and safe new front entrance and organize the deep and narrow backyard as a private sanctuary.

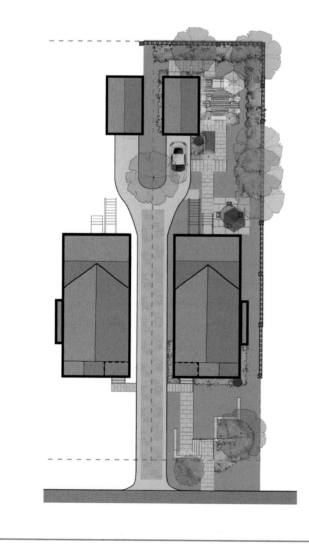

above • Prior to the improvements, the only access to the front door was by walking down the single-car driveway. Now a short bluestone walkway leads directly to the front door and a sunken terrace space enclosed by low stone walls.

above • Custom latticework panels attached to the garage screen the garden space from the driveway and provide vertical surfaces for climbing vines.

right • The rear garden, designed with privacy in mind, had an 8-foot fence along its perimeter but needed partitioning within to create separation between shared backyard spaces. A platform deck nestles against the wall of the garage to bring a sense of seclusion from the "attached" neighbor.

A curving path entices us to look around the corner to see what's there. The handsome barn overlooks a cobble-edged crushed stone driveway, framed and softened by trees.

above · Driveways take up a lot of space so it's important to make them attractive and functional. Here, long planks of concrete bring a handsome garden experience right up to the car door.

left · The scale of the stone pavers that edge this driveway provides an attractive counterpoint to the brick surface, while beautifully manicured rectangles of lawn add fresh splashes of green to break up the hardscape.

Turning a Driveway into a Garden

Our driveways take up a lot of space on our properties. What happens when a driveway is designed to be a beautiful garden, even if it's just for cars? In this large California property, the approach from the street is punctuated with handsome planters atop street number signs to either side to create a clear sense of arrival. Silvery santolina bushes billow softly at the base of columnar junipers and eucalyptus trees. A wooden fence to one side beckons the traveler onward, toward the house.

right • Carefully pruned hedges create a cloudlike surround for a parking area.

below • From the moment of entry, with no hint of house, a driver experiences this entire property as though it were a garden. A concrete curb keeps the crunchy driveway surface from migrating into the plantings.

Making Tracks

Like many once-common things whose modern-day replacements proved expensive or environmentally unsound, driveway paving strips are back in vogue. Paving strips are bands of paving materials just wide enough for a car's tires and can be made of recycled, poured, or dimensional concrete, thick stone pavers, cobblestones, brick, or gravel. The strips' surrounds can be planted in low, tough ground covers that can stand heavy foot traffic as people get in and out of vehicles. Best of all, these plantings act as pervious sponges so that water runoff doesn't overwhelm storm drains in the street.

1. Tire tracks allow a small vehicle like a golf cart or a larger maintenance vehicle to access the pool garden. Hydrangea, grasses, iris, and catmint all soften the irregular pattern of the cut-stone paths. 2. A gravel driveway meanders through a copse of trees to follow a stone wall to the house. 3. Different styles, shapes, and colors of concrete pavers are carefully designed to make it clear where people can walk and cars should go. The driveway's center strip, planted with thyme, breaks up the monotony of pavers and reduces runoff.

OPEN-AIR

You can make a living, dining, lounging — or even sleeping — space outside,

just as you do inside.

ROOMS

Getting Some Air

What does it take to make a room? You need four walls, a floor, and a ceiling. The space outside of your house is similarly defined. Walls can be made of stone, wood, stucco, or even hedging. The flooring might be durable concrete pavers, decking, or grass underfoot. The ceiling can be a porch roof, a pergola, or even the vast sky and stars above. You don't have to be an architect to make yourself an open-air room!

While an outdoor room can be just about anywhere on your property, the most traditional is an attached porch. As a part of the house itself, a porch usually sits under an extension of the roof and so it is well protected from the elements. It abuts at least one wall of the house and is often built at the same floor level as inside, so it's easy to move in and out of it. A porch can sit in the front, side, or back of the house, be narrow or wide, and be open or screened to keep out insects. This is the place where you can really live in the out-of-doors; where comfortable wicker or teak furniture with overstuffed pillows draws you out to a cool, shady spot.

Unless protected by an awning or shade structure, a deck or patio sits out under the stars. Constructed of wood, steel, or recycled materials, a deck is an extension of the house that can be built on top of a roof, to the side of a building, or even on the ground as a low platform. A patio is usually a level piece of ground on which a paved surface sits. It can extend the inside of a house out into the landscape as a large threshold for seating or act like a floating island in the midst of plantings or lawn. Paving options are plentiful.

top right · An outdoor nook, complete with parasols, lanterns, and couches, feels like it's been carved out of a dense grove of tall bamboo.

bottom right · A hedge of spiring arborvitae and a handsome magnolia tree form the walls of this comfortable outdoor room. Cozy furniture, a water garden, and perennial plantings of bee balm, iris, and bluestar draw the proud owners outside.

A blue-and-white striped carpet makes this outdoor terrace feel like it's indoors—except for the view!

Open-air rooms can also be constructed around swimming pools, hot tubs, and even outdoor showers —anywhere water can be enjoyed. A hard surface underfoot usually helps to keep wet feet from tracking dirt or grass clippings everywhere. Sometimes you might prefer an outdoor room with a verdant soft carpet underfoot. A well-clipped lawn or mossy glade offers a spot for picnicking or leisurely lounging on the grass.

These days, sheds are used for tool and garden-equipment storage, animal shelter, or even as a getaway space for work or for play. These mini-houses, when well designed, draw the eye and the foot, attracting children and the child in all of us to snuggle in for a while.

Porches

A porch feels simultaneously like a part of the house and a part of the landscape; it's a place perched somewhere in between. You can entertain, dine, and even sleep out on a porch, feeling close to the elements from a protected place.

Because most porches are not insulated structures that are built to withstand the weather, materials need to be weather-resistant, thoughtfully detailed, and built to last. Since rain and snow can accumulate on its roof, a porch needs to adhere to appropriate moisture-proofing, flashing, and guttering standards to keep water where it belongs: outside the structure. Rain chains and gutters can deposit water into rain gardens, but choosing local hardwoods like cedar or exotic woods like ipe or mahogany and finishing them with a moisture-proof stain will help maintain the structure, no matter the weather event.

top right • **A small side porch that sits amongst beautiful plantings is perfectly sized to be a breakfast room.**

bottom right • **This front porch feels both private and public at the same time. It is tucked under the eaves and opens out to a beautiful garden, but it is reached by a concrete path that links it directly to the street.**

Doric columns support the roof that offers protection from the elements for these lucky homeowners. Are you inside or are you outside? A bit of both.

Caulking joints to keep water from getting inside any structures is imperative with this kind of indoor-outdoor environment.

Similarly, you need to think about moisture issues as you choose your porch flooring. Mortared stone or brick works well outside, as does stained concrete. Wood finished with either a clear stain or a deck paint can hold up under rigorous weather conditions; with proper maintenance you'll enjoy your porch for years to come.

SCREENED PORCHES

On a hot summer's day, who doesn't love just curling up with a good book on an old settee in a screened porch with an overhead fan moving the air around? It feels just right. You're protected from the elements and marauding insects as you look out through a shimmering screen that turns the view into an abstraction of itself.

A well-designed screened porch can serve as a protected outdoor dining, living, play, and even sleeping room. With a solid roof overhead, either floor-to-ceiling screens or screens over well-caulked half-walls, and stone or wood flooring underfoot, a screened porch lets you live in the out-of-doors from late spring through early fall. Just be sure to screen the space between the floorboards to keep the mosquitoes out!

top right • People with screened porches often move in for the summer. Being so close to nature while the weather's good is like camping, except that a full kitchen and working stove are close at hand.

bottom right • Supporting posts help to frame distant views, breaking the landscape into parts the way a delicate folding screen does.

facing page • The extra-high ceiling of this screened porch helps cooling summer breezes waft in; a ceiling fan suspended from the beam helps as well.

Decks

Much like a porch, a deck is a floored structure that adjoins a house, but without the overhead protection of a roof. Because they perch on top of or at the edge of a landscape, decks can seem to float on high, perfect for basking in the sun or relaxing under the stars. Some decks sit on supporting posts; others cantilever beyond.

When designed thoughtfully, railings not only protect people from falling over the edge but also enable viewers to see through to the landscape below. Make sure to adhere to local building codes as you design your railing. Standard heights, spacing, and diameters of openings create a belt of safety around your deck.

above • Swimming pools need a dry walking surface surrounding them. This pool deck is made of wood to match the screen fencing and planter that double as the perimeter barrier around this narrow property.

left • A platform deck rests at lawn level, almost like you're floating on air. The nearby water element is a handrail that doubles as a water rill; we like to call it a "handrill."

right • Even a very low and simply designed deck feels like a special place to sit. The deep blue of the chairs makes this corner look invitingly cool and refreshing.

below • A deck is as much a part of the architecture as the rest of the house. Here, the picket fencing that encloses this high deck is visually repeated in the wall that conceals the storage area underneath.

Outdoor Living at Its Best

Ottawa landscape architect John Szczepaniak is the master of outdoor living spaces on small properties. On only a third of an acre, he has managed to shoehorn a swimming pool, living and dining area, and elegant gardens, all the while maintaining the clients' need for privacy from their neighbors all around. The home's mahogany posts seem to grow upward from the steps and decking, bringing needed harmony to a small space. The structure of the shoji-like topper on the privacy fence also echoes the decking.

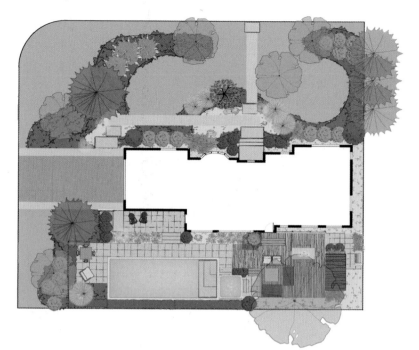

facing page • A tight backyard is no impediment to good design. Here, a wooden deck becomes the floor of an outdoor living room, while steps lead up and down to hot tub and swimming pool.

above • Lighting on steps is vital to safe passage, especially near pools.

right • Shoji-screen-like panels lit from within create a dramatic backdrop for the dining area.

Patios

A patio is an outdoor living space that sits directly on the ground. Often built adjacent to a house or other structure, a patio is usually made of some kind of paving material that makes a clean, level surface underfoot, allowing furniture and people to move around freely in this open-air room in the landscape.

Patios are defined as paved areas that adjoin a building, but they can also be built as courtyards at the center of a complex of buildings. Favored in southern climates as a means to regulate sun and shade throughout the day, these courtyards bring light and air and offer a realm of quiet seclusion for their users.

above • While a lawn can be a perfectly good surface on which to place comfortable outdoor furniture, it's easier on the person mowing the lawn if there's a more permanent solution: in this case, a small stone terrace that sits toward the corner of the garden.

Random-patterned granite stepping stones meander informally to a slightly raised bluestone terrace bounded in cobblestones. The little barnlike building then enjoys an open-air room of its own, far away from the main house.

Freestanding brick walls provide enclosure, seating, and a place for pots. Imagine how much less appealing this terrace would be if all the greenery were removed, both inside and outside the walls.

With materials available to suit all budgets and aesthetic preferences, adding a patio is one of the simplest routes to enjoying your yard more and making the most of the space you have. Whether tiny or expansive, sun-drenched or shaded, a patio presents an opportunity to create an outdoor living area customized to the way you want to live. With dining furniture for outdoor entertaining or private al fresco meals, or lounge chairs for reading and catnapping, you can expand your home's footprint to make more space for your favorite activities. An urban patio immersed in greenery and container plantings feels like a refreshing refuge in the city, while a beautifully hardscaped terrace can lend definition and structure to a rustic setting.

To ensure a feeling of continuity between indoors and out, make sure the design complements the style of your house, perhaps echoing an architectural line or detail, as in the case study on p. 70.

above • Different than natural stone, concrete pavers are an inexpensive patio and walkway solution. Because they tend to absorb rather than reflect light, pavers can be broken up with plantings, stones, or water features to reduce passive heat gain in warm climates and to soften their effect.

This pea gravel terrace is not only a low-maintenance lawn alternative, but it also allows rain to percolate to the roots of the hydrangea, crabapple tree, and gardens.

Paving Options

How you choose to pave your terrace is bound only by your imagination. Traditional materials like brick, bluestone, sandstone, and flat fieldstone are now augmented by contemporary concrete applications, such as concrete pavers, tinted poured concrete, and stamped concrete in a host of patterns. Loose stones and aggregates are also popular paving options, in part for their low cost, but also because they can filter water right into the soil.

TAMPED AGGREGATE

POURED CONCRETE

NATURAL STONE PLANTED JOINTS

BRICK WITH CONCRETE DETAIL

CUT BLUESTONE SQUARE SLABS

STONE CRACKED ICE PATTERN

Clean Lines, Bold Design

Landscape architect John Szczepaniak created this formal Asian-themed garden for an Ottawa couple in a suburban setting. Repurposing first-generation interlocking pavers from the 1980s and giving them some fresh zing with contrasting black granite, he created frames underfoot to highlight different areas throughout.

To the rear of the property, a handsome covered porch steps down to a dining patio, where Szczepaniak placed a square of black granite like a carpet underneath the table. Plantings in a restrained yet dramatic color palette emphasize the Asian feel of this energizing space.

above • A square marks the nexus of three
paths. Plantings of trimmed boxwood and
lacy goatsbeard create clean lines and
graded layers that provide a counterbalance
to the paving.

right • John's signature lighted screen
creates a vertical focal element in a narrow
yard. Finding ways to line up axes and
provide symmetrical framing in a small
space brings order and clarity to this
property.

facing page • There's no doubt about where
to place the dining table. The dark granite
pavers form an outdoor carpet, overtopped
by two large shade trees.

Lawns

When designed thoughtfully, your lawn can function as an open-air room that works as well for lounging and entertaining as it does for play. Grassy areas allow for a place where kids can kick a ball around, play tag, make a fort, or do somersaults. As with a glade in a forest, a lawn also serves to bring light and air into the property. Design your lawn as a "pool of space"—a continuous surface that is framed, like a swimming pool, by a clear edge. This will turn what seems like a leftover area into a handsome focal point of your landscape.

above • Lawn that runs right up to the front of a house can be featureless and boring, but this design softens and blends the transition with grassy plantings and pavers.

above • While many are trying to remove their lawns, this design presents a clear argument for some to stay. A well-edged expanse of grass can unify a complex landscape like this one.

left • A footpath leads to a very small but inviting pool of lawn that makes lounging and stargazing irresistible.

Low retaining walls define this square lawn as a garden room furnished with perennial plantings, a corner fountain, large shade trees, chaise longues, a glass-topped table and chairs—and a magnificent view.

Pools

A swimming pool can be designed as a handsome horizontal focal point that organizes the spaces around it. Most pools are formed from concrete shells topped by stone coping that acts as a frame for the water. If the pool is painted a dark color, like gray or black, the water reflects the sky; if painted turquoise to match the sky, then the two can seem to meld together as one. Both are attractive effects.

These days, pools are usually formed using a shotcrete method that allows different shapes and edgings to be formed. Another important development in pool design is the automatic pool cover, which works on a rectangular-shaped pool to keep children safe, intruders out, heat in, and evaporation to a minimum. The covers also help to reduce chemical use.

Chlorine Alternatives

Because chlorine by-products are linked to higher incidences of asthma, miscarriages, and cancer, new greener methods of disinfecting pools are also changing the way people swim. Ozonators combined with in-floor cleaners keep water clean with a minimum of chemical treatment. Saltwater pools are also popular, designed to reduce microorganisms to a safe level. Ultraviolet disinfection systems add a layer of protection by oxidizing organic contaminants.

above • Clean rectangular lines of stone coping turn this place for swimming into a focal point reflecting the sky. Ornamental grasses surround a spreading tree that's reflected in its still waters.

above • With the press of a button, an automatic pool cover glides into action. Not only is increased safety a big benefit, but also limiting evaporation means water is conserved. Long wide steps into the pool double as seats—basking places on a very hot day.

right • We designed this mountaintop pool with dark, gray, plaster finish to match the stone and reflect the sky.

below • The horizontal wooden slats of the fence are echoed in the decking that serves as the pool terrace for this combination pool and hot tub. Bluestone coping surrounds the pool but disappears into the silvery-gray of the cedar planking.

HOT TUBS & SPAS

For those of us living in northern climates, a hot tub is one of the best ways to relax in the out-of-doors, especially in the dead of winter. Some tout the therapeutic benefits from spray jets that can be set to massage different parts of the body. With temperatures as high as 104°F, these small pools can be built of wood with staves (like a barrel), shotcrete, or one piece stainless steel or acrylic and are powered by wood, gas, or electricity. Solar hot water systems are also possible in certain climates.

Whatever style hot tub you select, make sure to locate it close to an area in your house with a bath or changing room. While some people prefer to place their hot tub under cover of a roof or pergola, others like to use it as a nighttime retreat under the stars. When easily reached, a hot tub acts as a warm and comfortable "away room," even in the most inclement weather.

The path to a spa should be easily maintained and shoveled. Putting hooks nearby for robes or towels is a small but important detail. It's also a wonderful viewing position onto the rest of your landscape, so installing night lighting can enhance your hot tub experience.

above · This in-ground spa, complete with automatic cover, incorporates hydrojets that ease back and neck pain. The retaining wall encloses the spa on three sides, directing one's eyes to the adjacent swimming pool and the view beyond.

above · Hot tubs can be an annoyance in an otherwise beautiful backyard landscape. This one sits nestled into corner walls and is masked from view by a garden at its feet. Best, though, is the ability to sit immersed in water as you look across a millstone water fountain to a beautiful view beyond.

left · A small in-ground spa sits in its own charming walled garden—just far enough away from the main house to make getting there an adventure!

OUTDOOR SHOWERS

There is a freedom that comes from showering in the out-of-doors. For those lucky enough to have a pool or pond on their property or a beach nearby, it's helpful to have access to an outdoor area to clean or towel off before setting foot inside. A simple showerhead, some paving underfoot, a way to drain the water, and a screen or fence that allows air to circulate easily are just about all you need.

top left · This wonderful wall composed of seashells gives outdoor bathing a rococo elegance. An old-fashioned showerhead pours water down on the lucky recipient, who can pick a banana when it ripens.

bottom left · Air circulation is always important to consider when installing an outdoor shower. Slatted wood partitions lend privacy while allowing cooling breezes in. Deep shelves provide a place for soap and shampoo.

below · We designed this stone shower wall that was inspired by stone alcoves in Kashmir, India. Arched insets like these can be both practical—holding shampoos and vases—and an aesthetic delight.

Sheds and Outbuildings

Sheds are little houses that serve a range of functions in our backyard landscapes. Toolsheds, chicken houses, gazebos, meditation huts, even an outdoor workroom are all typical uses of a shed. Often designed to be a mini-version of the larger residence, a shed can be located near the main house or at a remote corner of the property. Either way, a shed can be a charming focal point or an alluring destination.

top right · **This little wooden shed houses an outdoor sauna nestled into a stand of tall trees.**

bottom right · **Setting your shed at the far edge of your property makes it feel as though it's remote, while drawing the eye— and foot—to visit. The pink door beckons!**

below · **A white-painted pool house that looks like a Greek temple sits at the head of a swimming pool, surrounded by plantings in white pots to match.**

above • Most of us have lawn mowers, gardening tools, outdoor play paraphernalia, and other items to store, but few of us do it as attractively as this elegant little wooden structure, which acts as a handsome wall to an adjacent outdoor kitchen.

right • Rooflines matter when it comes to little buildings like this burnt-orange painted shed. The trim lines of a hipped roof finished in cedar shingles sit like a hat over this sweet structure, whose black-lined windows, door, and threshold form a friendly face.

above • A charming meditation hut sits over a small round pond built of self-weathering steel, fed by a "handrill" designed by JMMDS. A sliver in the steel wall allows water to fall into another curving rill set as a focal element into the ground.

left • Star shapes cut into the wall of this handsome shed both puncture and punctuate in an unusual way.

A Potting Shed

Designer Mike Eagleton created the perfect potting shed—every gardener's dream—for his Denver client. In the tiny space, he created open shelving for pots and watering cans, bins for compost and soils, and drawers for implements. The all-important sink sits below a window sited at just the right height for viewing out into the garden, and a French door with mullioned windows lets in light, air, and views.

top right • Everything in its place—even the shovels and spades hang from high pegs.

bottom right • A pull-out bin with scooper sits full of potting soil, at the ready.

below • Awning windows are hinged at the top and open outward to allow for ventilation even during a light rain. Shelving and counter space were designed to be just at the perfect working height.

Shade Structures

As our globe heats up and more and more people face drought conditions, regulating the light overhead in our open-air rooms is vital to our enjoyment of nature. Retractable awnings allow homeowners to protect what's beneath from sun and rain as needed; openwork pergolas baffle and break up the sun's rays, while letting weather and cooling breezes through. Handsome patterns of light are cast upon the furniture and floor below; when combined with leafy vines, an overhead garden or orchard is created. Place your dining table underneath a grape arbor, and pluck away!

right • Grapevines provide shade against a building and are supported by an arbor formed of wooden pillars overtopped with steel struts that hold the rampant twiners.

below • Fabric tents are being used more and more for residential outdoor rooms. The domed skeletal structure of this tent not only casts cooling shade but is also a sturdy shelter from the rain. With integrated lighting, it's primed for evening gatherings around the rough-hewn stone table.

A long walkway is composed of white rafters held up by posts and beams. The resulting shadows change throughout the day.

right · Corten steel retaining walls hold up lawn panels, behind which a shady sitting nook nestles nicely beneath a handsome wood shade trellis. A frosted roof panel filters the sunlight and protects from the rain.

below · Nylon "sails" overhead provide shade with dramatic flair, at a minimal cost.

The leftover structure of an old corncrib provides a kind of lathhouse that is now covered with wisteria vine, making for a romantic getaway spot on a large property.

Protection from the Sun

Landscape designer Lisa Port of Banyon Tree Design Studio designed a cutting-edge shade structure for her Seattle clients, right in their front yard. She screened the 20- by 25-foot space from the sidewalk and street using narrow wooden fencing set horizontally and then underscored the corner with tall steel posts topped with pergolas. Canvas shade screens join house and pergolas to create a comfortable sitting space, no matter the weather. Steel planters, a bubbler of stone, and handsome plantings work together to make a dynamic garden that feels both private and spacious, despite its location and size.

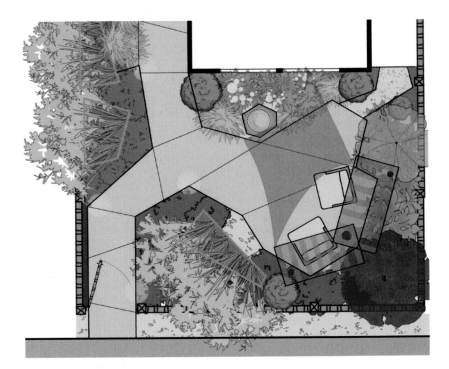

left · To bring harmony to a small property like this one, designers like to control the number of materials, colors, and textures that are used. Here, the same powder-coated metal color is used for the furniture, shade structures, and planter boxes, and it melds well with the fountain, paving, and fencing hues.

A carefully calibrated shade structure really can work. Between the shade tents and the slats, sitting in the hot late-afternoon sun becomes palatable.

WALLS,

When outdoor spaces are outlined by a wall, fence,

FENCES,

or hedge, they turn into places we seek to inhabit.

and HEDGES

Enclosures

An enclosure, like a wall, fence, screen, or hedge, defines and designates an outside area as special. Such boundaries have always played an important functional role in the landscape: to keep livestock in and intruders out. These days, an enclosure can also be used to delimit property lines, close in a hazard like a swimming pool, and create privacy where needed.

An enclosure also acts to extend the walls of the house out into the landscape. It's strange but true: An enclosed space feels larger than a similar area lacking such definition. Perhaps it's because a fenced yard feels marked out as special, with clear edges and an entrance gate or threshold.

There are many ways to create enclosures in your landscape. Walls, built of stone, concrete, or other masonry materials, bring a solid structural presence to a front or back yard. Wooden, steel, or bamboo fences sit more lightly on the land and are less expensive to erect, but they don't last as long as their masonry counterparts.

Hedges are the least expensive means of enclosing a landscape. Evergreen or deciduous, tall or low, hedges can be effective living screens for a variety of settings. Gateways create visual and actual breaks in an enclosure, allowing passage into the delineated realm. Railings are low post-and-rail structures designed to keep people from falling over an edge, especially on stairways or around high decks. The simplest kind of enclosure—an edging—separates plants or garden beds from pathways or lawns in a useful and attractive way.

above • A single wooden chair and ottoman sit in the crook of a handsome stone wall, carving out space for contemplation and a quiet cup of tea.

right • A rose-covered arbor marks the entry to this backyard paradise, delighting visitors with the fragrance of flowers and petals strewn along the stepping-stone entry path.

above • An old millstone serves as breakfast table in a corner of a low-walled terrace. Wooden stools sit at just the right height for dining while taking in the marvelous view.

left • This 6-foot-high wooden fence not only brings needed privacy between properties, but it also acts as a handsome backdrop to borders, trees, and climbers. Note the inlay detailing on the focal panel and the attractive black-green color.

Walls

Walls are powerful visual extensions of the architecture of your house into the landscape. They can be structural or ornamental and serve different purposes in the landscape. Structural walls are often tasked with retaining soil. Where the ground slopes, but a level area is needed, retaining walls are added to terrace the area. Freestanding walls are above the ground and can be seen from both sides. Sometimes these provide backdrops to gardens, define the edge of the property, or frame an opening for a driveway or path.

An interesting form can give walls greater character. Straight walls are practical, direct, and efficient. Curved walls, with their softer flow, can be playful, meandering, or sensuous. Tall walls that you can't see over or where a lot of soil is being retained can feel intimidating. A friendly height for a wall is one that allows a neighborly view between houses.

Materials and finish details can make all the difference. Stucco or stone, mortared or dry stacked, round or square stone, natural or cut stone cap, stucco texture and color—there are countless details to incorporate to give a wall your own personal touch.

top right · Dry-laid stone walls are an ancient form of enclosure, built originally to use up excess material, delineate boundaries, and keep in livestock. These days, we enjoy them for their beauty and sense of history.

bottom right · Even a house wall can become part of an outdoor enclosure, especially when it is as attractive and special as this one. Nine small square porthole-like windows form a grid of openings on this window wall.

above · This owner made a garden out of a handsome entry sign, whose style matches the house beyond. The yard's billowing gardens provide a refreshing contrast to the self-weathering steel.

left · Low retaining walls attractively solve a grade issue in this front yard. The designer kept plantings away from the low walls, immersing them in lawn for easy access for people to sit and children to climb on them.

STONE WALLS

Many of us are lucky to live where natural stone is plentiful. Whether flat or rounded, granite, gneiss, schist, sandstone, or limestone, a stone wall made out of what's local looks great because it is in keeping with the natural landscape. And there are many ways to build with stone. You can use flat fieldstones to face a wall or to create a built-up surface. Joints between the stones can be fully mortared, partially mortared (hidden joints), or dry laid, where no mortar is used at all. Make sure you employ an experienced mason to get the best results.

above • You can make stone walls in a number of different ways. This one uses stone veneer on a concrete block base—complete with limestone cap—as a retaining wall.

This freestanding wall inscribes an arc that encloses part of a driveway. With such a steep dropoff below the wall, local building codes mandate that there be a 40-inch-high turned-up edge for safety.

above · The walls of this outdoor kitchen, capped with bluestone, extend the living space into the out-of-doors. The metal chimney of a pizza oven sits kitty-corner, ready for action.

right · This dry stone wall was built without mortar. Large hewn stones cap the top and form treads for the steps that flow between the retaining walls.

SEATING WALLS

A seating wall is a masonry wall built at a height and depth to provide a place to sit. Retaining and free-standing walls alike can deliver a solid bench. Since stone can be cold to the touch, seating walls can be made to feel more comfortable when enhanced by a wooden seat or cushions, or when painted in light colors or softened by cascading plants. Typical seat heights can be as low as 12 inches and as high as 30 inches (more of a leaning height), with the usual height being 18 inches or so from the ground.

right · Most of us love nothing more than settling into a comfortable corner bench. This one, made of tinted concrete, is softened by vines and seat pillows and is overtopped by a lush pergola.

below · Freestanding concrete walls provide a corner for sitting by the handsome oblong fire pit of the same material. The wooden platform deck seems to float on the trim lawn, while wooden chairs offer a comfortable back for nestling.

Walled Garden

A grade change in this front yard posed a challenge to designer Maggie Judycki and her client, who'd recently had knee surgery. Judycki's elegant solution involved adding low stone walls and a smooth flagstone walkway. To break up the line from the house to the street, the stairs are placed at a right angle to the path. With low risers and deep treads, along with the sturdy handrail, the steps are designed for safety, but their attractiveness belies their practicality.

right • The lights installed under the capstones of the wall illuminate the steps for safe nighttime walking.

below • Crafted by the same mason (and using the same stone) as the house, the walls are low enough for extra seating during the annual ice cream social, as well as for acting as a favorite balancing and climbing spot for neighborhood children.

Wall Materials

Walls define a space. Whether they are freestanding to screen or divide a space or retaining to create levels in your garden, walls make landscapes more interesting and dynamic. You can sit on them, install plants that will climb up them, or create curves or angles with them. There are a multitude of contemporary and traditional products to choose from. Make sure to build a foundation that is appropriate to your climate and use a licensed contractor to install walls that are higher than 24 inches.

NATURAL FIELDSTONE
$
- Local rounded or flat fieldstone dry laid or with hidden mortared joints

PRECAST BLOCK
$
- Self-locking, stackable concrete blocks come in many colors, textures, and sizes

TOOLED AND STACKED
$$
- Cut stone that is built up with dovetail joints

STUCCO
$$
- Formed concrete or built up with concrete blocks and stuccoed in place

STONE VENEER
$$$
- Poured or block concrete base under veneer stone mortared in place

TILE VENEER
$$$
- Concrete wall with tile veneer

NATURAL FIELDSTONE

STUCCO

PRECAST BLOCK

TOOLED AND STACKED

STONE VENEER

TILE VENEER

Fences

Fences have distinct personalities of their own, whether they are mainly functional or more decorative. When a property needs a fence, it can be an opportunity to make it a feature—something special in the landscape.

An open-patterned fence is often used when separation is needed but privacy is not. Picket and split-rail fences are light and delicate. Solid fences provide privacy and security. These no-nonsense enclosures don't need to be plain; there are many materials, colors, patterns, and finish details to add interest.

Fences often emphasize straight lines—vertically and horizontally—in the landscape. Yet a fence needs to address the slope of the ground. Sections of fencing can either step up or down or slope to follow the grade. Following a curve, as along a road, the sections can zigzag perpendicular to each other, for a crisp look. Fences with curved sections must be custom designed, adding a tailored look to any landscape.

Materials, colors, and patterns bring variety. For wooden fences, the scale and size of the posts and boards make a difference; the heartier the posts and boards, the stronger the fence. Weather-resistant woods are the best choice if a natural finish is desired. Painting or staining can offer different finished looks, each with its own maintenance needs.

Patterns in fences vary from the spindles of a wrought-iron fence to the tops of pickets to the toppers of stockade fences. Lattice, cutouts, or custom patterning in the topmost section of a fence can bring a decorative element to a landscape. A good rule is to have the top pattern be no more than one-third of the overall height of the fence.

above • Leaving some space between wooden boards helps to provide light and air to the plants adjacent to it. The 2-foot topper provides an openwork frame that adds height and gives presence to the clean white look of this fence.

right • These days, horizontal board fences are popular, especially when enclosing contemporary houses and buildings. Notice how the steel railings on the porch and the wood struts on the house facade echo the dark brown fencing without mimicking it.

above • This tall
board fence moves
down the slope in
graduated steps,
while the plantings
follow the slope
in front of it. Its
height provides
complete privacy to
those who gather
around the fire.

right • This house
was built as a Swiss
chalet, so the
fencing around the
air-conditioners
needed to suggest
the style as well.
Painted a warm gray,
the vertical boards
were cut with a
jigsaw to vent the
air-handling units
and knitted together
with a simple
board cap.

You can add a living layer to your fence by planting a vine nearby that can twine its way across it. Grape and hops vines are vigorous growers, as are flowering favorites like clematis, trumpet, and wisteria. When you plant climbers on a solid board fence, you'll need to provide small nails or screws for twining; on openwork screen, the vines will usually weave through openings on their own. Another way to veil a tall fence is to plant an espalier—usually a fruit tree that's been trained to a flat plane—in front of it.

right • A lyrical ornamental iron gateway provides the structure for a climbing clematis vine in flower. How beautifully it melds with the soft peach color of its house beyond.

below • Low pasture fencing skirts a wildflower meadow, where orchard trees rise forth out of white Queen Anne's lace and grasses. This kind of fence keeps horses and other livestock in, while bordering a country lane.

above · Screen fencing allows airflow into the backyard while offering privacy. The wooden lattice fence supports the growth of a vine and matches another that screens the dining terrace from the street.

left · A high metal fence keeps intruders out while allowing visual access to the adjacent field. A low concrete curb acts both as fence footing and retaining wall, while the arrowlike finials deter trespassers.

Giving Structure to the Garden

Landscape designer M J McCabe shows us just how important an attractive enclosure can be in a backyard landscape. The handsome square-lattice fence is sturdy enough to withstand Connecticut's snowy winters, while bringing a consistent structure to the mixture of trees, shrubs, perennials, and bulbs that are planted within it.

top left • Yellow and white daffodils—so welcome after a long, cold winter—light up the garden in early spring.

top right • June brings a cacophony of colors—salmon poppies, multi-colored bearded iris, hardy pink orchids, purple allium, and the violet-blue sprays of spring-blooming butterfly bush in the background.

bottom left • Late-blooming spires of blue salvia and fading Joe Pye weed offset the multi-tonal greens and browns of this autumnal garden.

bottom right • Snow blankets the garden, emphasizing plant form and structure rather than color.

Hedges

A hedge planting is one way to build an enclosure without breaking the bank. It can be made of evergreen materials, like an arborvitae hedge; deciduous plants, like lilac, hornbeam, or privet hedge; or even a mixed planting that combines both.

Some hedging materials, like privet or boxwood, look best when sheared or hand-pruned regularly to maintain an appropriate size and breadth. Other live screening looks good when left to grow to its natural height, such as lilac and rhododendron hedges.

Mixed hedges add variety in color and texture; imagine evergreens growing with climbing roses and a contrasting foliage shrub. Given the right growing conditions, and depending on the plant selection, most hedges will mature quickly.

above • Fastigiate (narrow and upright) forms of trees are useful as tall hedging material in restricted side yards such as this one. Hornbeam may lose its leaves in winter but it has a feathery foliage and filigree-like branching structure that makes it a pleasing sight year-round.

left • Because it is so easy to prune, privet makes a satisfying hedging material that can be trimmed into architectural or curving shapes. In this garden, the hedge acts as a soft and inexpensive deciduous wall that encloses the open-air room enjoyed by the homeowner.

For this plant lover, the garden acts as a hedge and the hedge as a garden. Here a mix of materials, colors, textures, and bloom periods all enclose this lawn while providing ongoing visual and horticultural interest. It helps to have a verdant, well-edged lawn as a base.

A low hedge of clipped evergreen boxwood tidily encloses a sculptural fountain. The boxwood's formality makes a nice counterpoint to the slightly wild spill of the white-blooming hydrangeas within.

Gateways

A gateway marks a threshold in the landscape. As a break in a wall or fence, the gate itself can be the highlight of the enclosure.

A gate is often continuous with its neighboring fence, built of the same materials and patterns, but with a different height or detailing to set it off as special. Sometimes gates want to look distinct from the fence or wall. Building a pergola or trellis overhead is a way to distinguish a gateway. Embellishing the entrance with a flowering vine signals the delightful garden experience ahead.

A nice detail is to allow the path material to slip under the gate, as an indication of the place to pass. If steps are needed near where the gate is placed, coordination is key. Stepping up or down while operating the gate can be tricky.

top right • Red-coated welded-wire panels, set as openwork in stained wood frames, provide an inexpensive way of maintaining views and airflow through both entry gateway and front fence.

right • A thick arched wooden gateway opens between white stucco walls to reveal a secret garden within. The small wrought-iron window, placed perfectly at head height, allows the owners to see who is knocking.

above left • A narrow arched doorway frames a view into a verdant walled vegetable garden. The unusual hexagonal fretwork piques our interest and limits our range of vision to just the stepping-stone pathway down the middle.

above right • An elegant moon gate beckons us to look first, then walk through the stone walls into this shingled house's backyard. The walls are made of rough-hewn ashlar stone, in contrast with the smooth, unpainted finish of the cedar gate.

left • A wattle fence offers a stark contrast to the gleaming white board fence beyond. Note the diagonal branches that brace the gate's frame and keep it square to the post so it's easy to open.

Railings

Railings are vital to our security in a landscape, helping to keep us from falling while on steps, decks, and balconies. They are particularly important as handholds in periods of inclement weather and as we age. They can lead a visitor physically and visually into a landscape, or they can seem to disappear to allow us to appreciate a view beyond.

Painted or natural, railings can complement adjacent gardens. Their pattern and rhythm can be a strong element in the landscape. When attached to a deck, a railing can interrupt our view of the world beyond. However, new cable systems provide enclosure while not interfering with our view. Always check local building codes that specify the conditions under which a railing must be incorporated.

above • A mahogany framework supports stainless-steel cables that meet the building code while allowing a view of the landscape beyond. A lightweight resin pot cast with a watering hole allows for watering with a hose without disturbing the blossoms.

Glass panels set into a sturdy frame help those who live on lakes or oceans contend with strong winds and the desire to view out. Keeping them clean is no small undertaking but is well worth the effort.

above • When you paint something black, it seems to disappear. Making sure that you follow building codes that regulate fence heights, materials, and details like the spacing between rails is imperative when you have steep drops like these.

right • This handsome painted openwork handrail is built with an intricate and unusual diagonal pattern. The crisp white of the window trim, handrails, and fascia board contrasts starkly with the chromium yellow of the plantings and siding.

Edging

When you edge your walkway, garden bed, or lawn area, you create a clean, crisp demarcation that satisfies our need for definition in a landscape. Like a molding strip or a border on a wooden floor, creating a belt around a space, however subtle, brings it into focus.

You can make an edging using a border of boxwood or other low hedge, cobblestone or brick, pressure-treated lumber on end, roofing tile, plastic edging, or even just a dug edge that separates bed from lawn—creating a continuous and distinctive line around a pool of space.

above • Self-weathering steel seems to emerge out of the concrete stairway, "growing" as it curves to contain a planting bed and define the edge of the lawn.

Bamboo can easily invade any garden where it's planted, unless a clumping form is selected. Strong, clean edging, like this 2-inch board on end, borders a drainage strip of river stones before ascending to a wooden deck.

above • Granite cobbles hold in pebbles both along a path and around a terrace, on which a simple picnic table rests for outdoor dining.

The least expensive edging is often
the most effective. A walkway
of grass is edged with a spade
to create a beautiful line that
looks wonderful with spilling and
billowing plantings adjacent to it.

Finished Edges

Just as piping or a band of grosgrain ribbon provides a clean finish to a seam on a dress, so an edge in a garden acts as a way to detail a design.

EXTRUDED CONCRETE EDGE

- Extruded concrete curbing creates a clean, flowing edge for this stabilized soil walkway. Concrete is fed into an extruding machine, then compacted and fed out through the chosen mold, with control joints cut every 3 feet.

COBBLESTONE EDGE

- Cobblestones provide a clean edge between lawn and other materials such as loose gravel or pavers. In colder climates, they need a deep long footing that keeps them from moving during freeze-thaw cycles. They can be placed horizontally or on edge, if supported underneath.

METAL EDGE

- Aggregate and peastone walkways need an edge to keep the fine stones from drifting into the garden or lawn. A metal edge is a slim, flexible option that lasts for a long time.

JAPANESE WOODEN EDGE

- Wood tree trunks placed on end provide an elegant edge that can vary in height and follow curves easily. Select a longer-lasting material like cedar or moisture-proof the ends that go into the ground.

PRECUT BLUESTONE EDGE

- A cut stone such as bluestone, granite, or limestone creates a satisfying edge, especially when it bands a contrasting or similar material.

EXTRUDED CONCRETE EDGE

COBBLESTONE EDGE

JAPANESE WOODEN EDGE

METAL EDGE

PRECUT BLUESTONE EDGE

PATHS AND

A well-designed path can lead you

on a journey of discovery through your property.

WALKWAYS

Path and Passage

Like a hallway that connects the different rooms of your house, a path through a landscape links different places on your property to each other. A formal entry walkway leads from the sidewalk to the front door; a semiformal cut stone path joins your dining terrace to the grill area; an informal stepping-stone path links gardens while keeping your feet dry; and a soft footpath defines the route from kitchen to the compost bin.

Depending upon its purpose, a path can be wide or narrow, straight or meandering, ramped or stepped, long or short. What's important is to make the journey through your property as interesting as the destination itself.

above • A labyrinth of carefully cut sandstone leads the seeker on a contemplative journey that helps cleanse the mind of other thoughts.

below • The clean lines of a concrete path lead visitors directly from the street to the front door and across the front yard to the driveway and garage.

An arbor is a verdant gateway
into this front-yard space.
Climbing hydrangea intertwines
with red climbing roses to
delight the senses and mark the
transition into the garden.

FORMAL PATHS

Without a paved walkway underfoot, we would track mud and debris right into our house. Choosing a walkway surface that is durable, not slippery, and easy to maintain (and shovel in northern climes) is essential to moving between the parts of our property that should be easily accessible throughout the year.

A formal path delineates the best route to our front, back, side, garage, or shed door. Often built wide enough for two people to walk side by side, a front walk can be curving or straight, depending upon aesthetic preferences. The choice of material can either match or contrast with the materials of the house. Natural stone, brick, poured concrete, or concrete pavers are just a few of the possibilities available to homeowners when they seek to build a formal path.

above · An expanse of square pavers in this front courtyard is interrupted with squares of baby's tears and palm trees. Note how the soft pinkish hue of the house matches the color of the paving material.

left · A concrete walkway can look modern and original when formed into pavers of graduating size separated by narrow strips of gravel (which also help to absorb rainwater).

facing page · A grand front gateway opens into a "vestibule" of mortared fieldstone that continues as a narrow path, moving visitors alongside a series of formal hedges and terminating in a handsome front porch.

Paths Underfoot

On this charming Seattle street of modest matching bungalows on small lots, one property really stands out because of its gardens and its paths. Billows of plantings tumble over street, sidewalk, and driveway, filling up every square inch of front-yard space that is not devoted to circulation.

Landscape designer Lisa Port understood the need to create privacy in this wide front yard, but she also wanted to give the homeowners a place to enjoy it by tucking a little terrace among the billowing plantings. She created a "bridge" built of decking to the yellow front door; it passes over the rain garden swale full of beach stones and wet meadow plantings below. Decomposed granite paths, edged in steel and inset with bluestone planks, run parallel to the house to the pervious terrace, topped with a charming yellow bistro table and chairs.

facing page top • A formal path of wooden decking takes you straight to the front door.

facing page bottom left • A decomposed granite terrace edged in steel holds yellow bistro chairs in this front yard garden.

facing page bottom right • In the semiformal path that runs along the front of this house, planks of cut stones are set into decomposed granite, echoing the decking on the bridge to the front door.

below • You can always tell who are the garden lovers in any given neighborhood.

SEMIFORMAL PATHS

Semiformal paths are useful when we want to keep our feet dry but don't need a continuous surface underfoot to do so. Cut stone or dimensional concrete pavers, separated by gravel, plantings, or grass, offer a less formal way to link house to garden or different parts of the garden to each other, and can be fun to design and to use.

Depending upon your manner of walking, you might choose a bigger or smaller stone size and space them so that it's easy to walk at a normal gait. Because the pavers are cut (usually as a square or rectangular), make sure that you place them to relate visually to the geometry of the house.

right • Cobblestones not only line this meandering path but also divide it up as rhythmic stripes between colorful stone pavers. Raising the edging on either side of the gently pitched path not only holds up the earth for plantings but also enables runoff to drain away toward the lawn.

bottom right • Brick is a versatile path material on its own or in combination with others. Here it is used both as filler and as "racing stripes" that lead you straight to the front door.

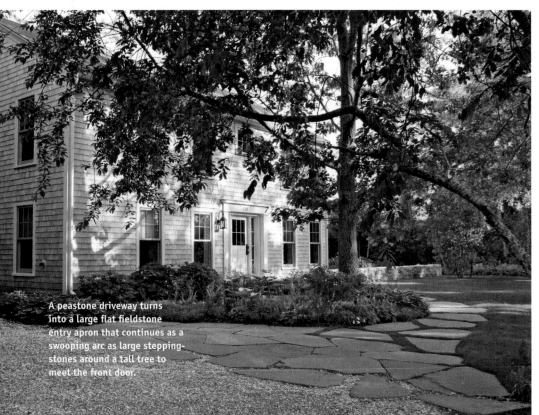

A peastone driveway turns into a large flat fieldstone entry apron that continues as a swooping arc as large stepping-stones around a tall tree to meet the front door.

Bluestone squares and rectangles follow a gentle curve through garden beds. Here, vinca, hostas, ferns, and white astilbes spill over the walk's edges. Grass fills the joints between the pavers.

Multiple Pathways

This beautiful California garden is built around a hierarchy of paths of local sandstone. Designed by Janet Lohman, the front garden weaves dry-tolerant plantings with gravel and paths. Two Buddhist pines (*Podocarpus* spp.) form a fulcrum to either side of the central path, mortared to take you directly to the front door. Offshoot stepping-stone paths weave their way through succulents and grasses; one goes to the driveway and one to a charming terrace that nestles against a tall vine-covered fence.

With its wide stone path and tawny mulch, this xeric (low-water) landscape captivates. Its simplicity of design allows the special features along the way—whether stones, plantings, or water feature—to sing.

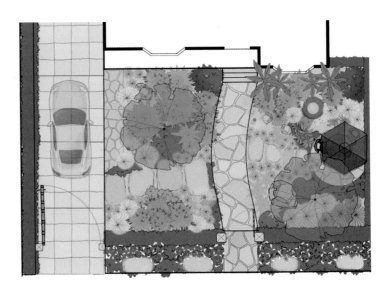

below • The front path, measuring 4 feet wide, offers a graceful way for two people to walk side by side to the front door.

above left · Wide sandstone steppers lead the visitor to an intimate patio made of the same material. Under the high fronds of a giant bird of paradise (*Strelitzia nicolai*), a glazed clay pot holds a bubbler of water to delight the ears.

above right · The little terrace invites us to sit under an eggplant-hued café umbrella, offering shade and a feeling of privacy in this front-yard garden.

right · An informal path leads to the formal driveway. Generously sized stepping-stones make for a more comfortable walk through the garden.

INFORMAL PATHS

Sometimes we want a simple way to move from one place to the other, but prefer an individual contemplative experience as we do so. Stepping-stones, like natural-cleft flat fieldstones or quarried granite or limestone, are easy to assemble and fun to follow. Spaced several inches apart, and often sized to fit an average foot, each stepping-stone should be placed the way you walk: right foot/left foot/right foot/pause. For ease of maintenance, sink each stone into a low ground cover or a lawn, so that a machine can easily mow right over them.

below • A narrow gardener's path through a thickly planted side yard enables someone to weed, water, and prune.

above • A boardwalk that leads across beach plantings feels good under bare feet, especially arriving at an outdoor shower built of the same material. Spacers between the silvery cedar planks allow water to drain through, and boards are easily replaced as they wear out over time.

above • Stone steps, created from flat-topped boulders, provide an informal path through a garden. Make sure to place a large landing stone at the departure and destination points, and break up the length somewhere in the middle with another large stone, to give the climber a break.

Stepping-Stone Technique

When stepping-stones are large enough, they can take the place of a more formal path, especially in climates that don't require snow removal in winter. Make sure to start and end every stepping-stone path with a large stone that acts as a threshold from which to view the whole experience. To make sure you provide the proper gait for your visitor, set stepping-stones about a wrist width apart. Think about how your feet move right, then left; right, then left along a path, and set your stones accordingly. Because we walk with our heads down on stepping-stone paths, it helps to place a larger stone every eight or so stones, one that allows people to place both feet on it, so they can slow down and notice where they are and where they're going. Finally, create a yin-yang relationship between most of the stones so that they feel connected to each other. Using these guidelines will ensure that the stepping-stone journey feels natural and enjoyable underfoot.

above • Even broken and quarried stones like these can be set in a satisfying way. Note the yin-yang relationship here: The smaller stone seems to nestle into the larger one to its left.

above • The general rule in stepping-stone placement is to set them 2 to 3 inches apart in a slightly staggered pattern to make strolling easy.

SOFT PATHS

Not all paths need to be paved. Sometimes merely mowing a way through a wildflower meadow or repeatedly tramping a trail through the woods is enough to link areas of our landscapes. A soft path offers an inexpensive, easy-care choice for busy homeowners on properties large and small. Good alternatives to paved paths include grass, bark mulch, pine needles, stabilized soil, and pea gravel. "Steppable" ground covers are also available, but are best for occasional foot traffic only.

above • Crunchy gravel underfoot makes for an inexpensive and permeable path material, here edged in natural stones and tree trunks.

right • Decomposed granite or limestone is an inexpensive underfoot material. Edge it with plantings, stone, or walls to hold the small-gauge stone in place.

facing page left • A plant lover's paradise is knitted together by a gravel path that meanders through its beds like a stream.

facing page right • A long grass path leads through deep perennial beds full of flowers. Make sure to keep the width the size of your mower, so that one swipe down the center is all it takes.

Path Materials

Depending upon your needs and your budget, a path can be an inexpensive or a costly element in your landscape. Here is a glossary of material choices and their relative costs to help you decide.

BARK MULCH
$
- Soft and quiet underfoot.
- Biodegradable material, should be refreshed with new mulch each year.
- Very easy to install.
- Can compact over time (which can create drainage problems).

PEASTONE
$$
- Permeable surface and comes in a variety of colors.
- Easy to transport into small areas.
- Stones may travel into the garden, so use an edge to retain it.

PRECAST PAVERS
$$$
- Widely available, durable, and easy to install with tight joints.
- Pavers come in a variety of patterns, colors, and textures.

BRICK
$$$
- Very widely available, durable, easy to install.
- Small size allows flexibility in creating curves and patterns.

CONCRETE
$$$$
- Can be formed into virtually any size or shape desired.
- Can be tinted and/or stamped with a pattern.
- Can have an aggregate, such as pebbles, added to create a nubbly texture.

CUT STONE SLABS
$$$$$
- Long-lasting material, comes in a variety of colors.
- Easy to sweep and shovel, so appropriate for a main walkway.

BARK MULCH

CONCRETE

PEASTONE

PRECAST PAVERS

CUT STONE SLABS

Steps and Stairs

Inside the house, we usually move efficiently and quickly between floors. Outside, people move up and down the landscape at a slower pace. Inclement weather brings safety concerns in the out-of-doors, so steps and staircases need to be built differently than their counterparts indoors. The general rule for landscape steps is to create deeper treads (14 inches as opposed to the 11 inches to 12 inches indoors) and shallower risers (5 inches to 6 inches as opposed to the 7½ inches indoors) to accommodate these concerns. Professionals use the following formula for landscape steps: Two times the riser plus the tread equals 26 inches to 27 inches.

above • A voluptuous, curving set of steps ending in a handsome stone pedestal entices us to move between upper and lower lawns. We imagine wedding ceremonies, concerts, and other special events taking place here.

below • These poured concrete steps show the deep tread and low riser of a typical landscape step. Notice how the walls, steps, and terrace flow continuously, as though completed in one pour.

above • Granite curbs set in threes provide steps up a grass-ramped slope through a forest garden.

We created steps down a steeply sloping backyard using a framework of self-weathering steel that holds in peastone treads. To the right is a steel handrail that holds water—we call it a "handrill."

135

LANDINGS

Landings give us a place to pause as we move up and down the different areas on our property. They are particularly important to break up a long run of stairs so that we may catch our breath and look ahead to the next landing.

top right • Use landscape lighting to prevent tripping hazards. The lights shown here illuminate the landings and draw attention to the subtle change in grade.

below • One large stone landing at the base of a long run of steps provides a place to stop before we move on to experience the terrace of brick. These small moves are critical to a safe and enjoyable journey through the space.

bottom right • This generous brick landing is both a pivot point, where one might turn right or left, and a space to pause and appreciate the house's gracious entryway.

Think of a landing outside your front entry as the counterpart to the foyer inside. This large square of herringbone-patterned brick set into a frame of bluestone gives space to pause before entering the house.

Bridges

A bridge is a structure that allows passage across a barrier or a gap. Often built of wood or steel, it might cross a river, ravine, or dry streambed, linking one shore to the other. Like a tunnel, which burrows through an obstacle rather than over it, a bridge is a continuation of a path where it otherwise might not be able to go.

above · These wide planks of wood are set in a staggered pattern, allowing passage across a sunken garden of birch trees underplanted with ferns.

right · A bridge over an elegant dry streambed serves as a drain for seasonal runoff in this yard.

facing page top · This front-entry-path bridge floats across a swale filled with river stones that act as a filter and dry well for excess rainwater.

facing page bottom · A simple arched bridge links woodland paths over a shallow stream. The bridge is made sturdy by its solid concrete foundation, which helps channel the stream under the bridge and into a small pond below.

PLANTINGS

Hardscapes are brought to life when you plant trees, shrubs, ground covers,

and vines, as well as flowering perennials and annuals.

And don't forget those edibles.

Planting Schemes

Design professionals divide landscape elements into two parts: hardscapes—the decks, walls, paths, terraces, and driveways that are permanent features of our property—and softscapes—the trees, shrubs, vines, flowers, and ground covers that live and change throughout the seasons and over the years. These softscape plants are the easiest and often least expensive way to make a quick and dramatic change to your landscape.

From a stately collection of trees to a vivid explosion of perennial plantings, plants can completely alter the character of your outdoor space. Providing utilitarian solutions for a wide range of design challenges, plants provide screening, surface water collection, wildlife habitat, and ground cover. Last but certainly not least, plants supply sustenance and satisfaction when we try our hand at growing our own food.

Plants are dynamic, changing through the seasons and over the years; they provide energy and excitement in the landscape. While a large boulder may stay in its place for many years, the same is not necessarily so for a plant. Most plants can be easily moved around. Shrubs can be reshaped or moved if need be and even mature trees can be cut down, and perennial beds can be reworked as often as necessary. Plants are the most malleable part of the landscape.

New gardeners benefit from starting small and investing in their own plant education. Careful observation can go a long way. Novices can learn a lot by keeping records of bloom times or by visiting other gardens to take notes on successful plant combinations. Or hire a gardening coach, join a garden club, or work one-on-one with a professional designer for the first few years.

above • The white bark of paper birch trunks melds beautifully with the white flowering perennials at its base, including asiatic lilies, Gaura (*Gaura lindheimeri* 'Stratosphere White'), shasta daisy (*Leucanthemum* 'Becky'), and 'White rain' Salvia (*Salvia nemerosa*).

above • Palette of greens: bamboo (*Phyllostachys*), Japanese forest grass (*Hakonechloa macra* 'Aureola'), and ground-covering Brass Buttons (*Leptinella squalida*).

above • Shasta daisies (*Leucanthemum* 'Becky'), black-eyed Susans (*Rudbeckia fulgida* 'Goldstrum'), white and purple phlox (*Plox paniculata* 'David' and 'Nicky'), shiny coneflowers (*Rudbeckia nitida* 'Herbstonne'), and ornamental grasses (*Miscanthus* spp.) were selected for their joyous profusion of blooms in time for an early August wedding at this Vermont garden. Learning the height, spread, and bloom period for your plantings helps you plan for the effect you want.

Bed Layouts

The shape of your beds sets the stage for your plantings. It also expresses the style of your garden. Whether they are symmetrically aligned or organically shaped, formal or natural, the beds will be most cohesive if they relate to the surrounding landscape and existing architecture.

Be sure beds are deep enough to plant in layers that ascend in height from front to back. Remember that beds of flowering shrubs and perennials provide the solid form that gives shape to the adjacent lawn.

right • One way to create bed layouts is to fill up the ground plane with plants. Here, happy tangles of roses, lavender, and Sticky Jerusalem sage (*Phlomis russeliana*) work their magic.

below • Simple, clean curves of evergreen spurge *(Pachysandra terminalis)* contrast elegantly with the lines and color of this historic home, while protecting the roots of an ancient maple tree.

A curving perennial border accomplishes three important goals: It brings color and beauty to this Vermont backyard, it echoes the curving lines of the swimming pond beyond, and it forms a backdrop for the fire pit deep enough so that no one can fall off the edge of the viewing terrace.

A Beautiful Rain Garden

A rain garden is a delightful way to solve the persistent problem of surface water runoff. Because more and more of the earth's surface is being paved or covered with human-made structures, the soil can't do its essential job of recycling rainwater. Instead, the water runs off all those paved surfaces—picking up contaminants such as oil, fertilizer, pesticides, and other pollutants as it goes—and carries it all to the nearest waterway or sewer drain.

You can keep rainwater out of overworked sewer systems and help prevent the pollution of our lakes and rivers. Direct the rainwater that lands on impervious surfaces like roofs and driveways to a planted infiltration basin right on your property. Deep-rooted plants utilize the water, and a healthy bed of soil with all of its microscopic organisms will break down harmful contaminants.

Rain gardens are a great place to use native plants, which evolved to fare well in your area without the fertilizers and pesticides that would impede microbial activity in the soil and contaminate the rainwater.

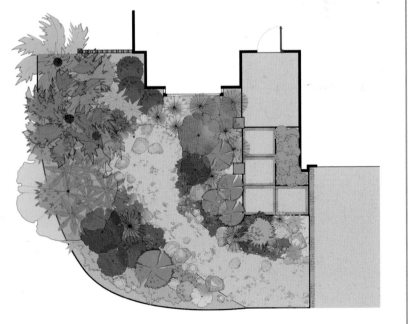

facing page • Designer Nancy Harrington of Evergreen Garden Designs created a handsome rain garden for her southern California client. She designed a dry riverbed that moves diagonally across the front yard, starting at the base of a pair of tall palm trees and widening out at the sidewalk and driveway. Planting beds to either side form the "shorelines" that soften the hardscape of the entry path and hold the steep slope and provide a strong and private edge to this corner lot.

top left • Stones in a variety of sizes, colors, and textures straddle "stream" and shore, just as they might in nature. The metal edge helps keep stones from migrating and also creates a beautiful line for the eye to follow back into the landscape.

top right • This xeriscape feels lush, while fulfilling the need for low water use in this dry part of the state. Easy-care plants like juniper, cape rush, gaura, geranium, sea lavender, and ground-covering ajuga allow more time to enjoy the garden than time spent maintaining it.

Trees and Shrubs

Trees and shrubs lend structure to the landscape. They provide shade, verticality, screening, and beauty. Whether deciduous or evergreen, they are stable forms in the garden year-round. Living for decades or even centuries, they are long-lasting legacies in the landscapes we create.

Trees are an essential component of our home landscapes, often contributing to comfort and a sense of place, although it needn't take a grove or a forest to make people feel at home. Many plains and southwestern states have a natural scarcity of trees. In climates like these, carefully selected specimen trees can make a strong statement.

Above most other landscape elements, trees and shrubs have the power to subdue the imposition of human-made architecture. Offering height, structural stability, and visual mass, trees can help to "settle" a built structure into its natural surroundings. Often the beauty and value of a neighborhood dwelling is related to the age and appropriateness of its trees.

Since trees can be such a prominent feature in the garden, their species, size, style, care, and placement should be carefully considered. Natural or habitat gardens benefit both visually and functionally from a selection of native tree species. Trees and shrubs with dependable, symmetrical habits are the best selection for formal spaces. Species with a season of flowering often fit well into ornamental gardens. Evergreens are the best option for year-round screening.

right • **A young Japanese white pine provides a lacy vertical contrast to the silvery stone and verdant plantings at its feet. Evergreen trees that retain their leaves or needles, like this one, bring some much-needed color through cold and harsh winters.**

left • A joyful statue, set in the corner of a tall wall, seems to give thanks to the overarching branches of this Japanese maple tree (*Acer palmatum* 'Dissectum'). The lime-green color of its leaves and its horizontal habit make this species a particular favorite.

below • When siting trees, think of the future—a mature tree, like this eucalyptus, can not only frame views from the house, but, when sited correctly, also provides cooling shade from the summer sun, acting as a natural air-conditioner.

STRUCTURE

Both trees and shrubs can act as a living wall to
screen, frame, or emphasize views. They can serve
as an alternative or complement to walls or fences,
offering softness, variability, seasonal color, and
beauty. Evergreens certainly provide the most consistent visual barrier, but combinations involving
fences, climbers, shrubs, and deciduous trees or large
shrubs can provide multiple layers of visual interest.

right • The open canopy of this Japanese maple tree acts as
a filigreed screen that makes the background terrace more
mysterious and enticing.

below • This formal garden showcases a beautifully branching
tree at its point; small trees and shrubs of varying sizes create
a richly textured effect.

The banyan (*Ficus microcarpa*) is a tropical shade tree with beautiful light gray bark and, in tropical and subtropical conditions, a great number of prop roots. Native to India, China, and Malaysia, this fig can grow to more than 50 feet high and has beautiful evergreen glossy leaves.

PRIVACY

Trees and shrubs also provide an inexpensive way to achieve privacy, whether as vertical screening between properties, as a hedged garden room by the house, or set off on their own. Tall evergreens planted close together provide the most seclusion but also cast the deepest shadows. Deciduous trees can be planted in rows for a leafy aerial hedge or as a loose grove whose thick planting depth blocks out undesired views. Of course, the larger the specimen you plant, the more quickly you'll achieve the privacy that you're seeking.

above • Orange Adirondack chairs converse together in a sunny nook overlooking a grassy hedge. A massive spruce tree adds a layer of privacy far above the 6-foot wooden fence.

left • A tall verdant yew hedge (*Taxus* sp.) insulates this front yard from road noise and traffic. Set back a generous distance from the street, the hedge leaves plenty of space for a simple yet elegant palette of plantings.

facing page bottom • Native serviceberry trees (*Amelanchier canadensis*) form a lacy screen to bring privacy to this home on a busy street. Birds love their berries, and the leaves turn a remarkable peachy-orange color in autumn.

right • Heritage River birch (*Betula nigra* 'Heritage') trunks exfoliate or shed their salmon-hued bark in attractive layers. These three form a mini-grove along the fence and add privacy and shade to this long, narrow backyard.

A Backyard Retreat

Seattle landscape architect Brooks Kolb created an elegant landscape to meld beautifully with a mid-century modern home built in 1962. The new owners wanted a private dining terrace on the east side of the house. Bands of white Texada concrete pavers alternate with fields of charcoal Texada to give interest to the flat plane around three sides of the house. A coffee table sits between yellow settees that meld beautifully with the Coral Bark maple, *Acorus* grass, and blue star creeper that are interwoven with Japanese-style plantings already planted around the house.

above · Charcoal Texada pavers cut to fit dovetail nicely with natural cleft stone stairs that wend their way up a planted hillside behind the couches. The repetition of mounded forms of different species brings harmony to this small garden.

facing page top · Mounding azaleas and a red Japanese threadleaf maple (*Acer palmatum* var. *Dissectum atropurpureum*) create the substructure of the white flowering Korean dogwood trees (*Cornus kousa*). Against the house, river-washed rock edges the walls, edged by existing concrete bands, softened by blue star creeper (*Isotoma fluviatilis*).

facing page bottom left · Chartreuse-colored outdoor couches sit happily on the ribbons of colored pavers. The pavers have an architectural finish and are hydraulically pressed and finished with beveled top edges.

facing page bottom right · The small-scaled Japanese stone lantern and water basin are almost dwarfed by the large trees and shrubs behind them, turning this long, narrow garden into a virtual rain forest.

COLOR

Green is just one of the many colors of trees. Blooms and fall foliage aside, the spectrum of available leaf colors is as broad as the rainbow. Many cultivars are specifically bred for color intensity. Japanese maples (such as *Acer palmatum* 'Bloodgood') are known for their rich red leaves. False cypress (*Chamaecyparis lawsoniana* 'Lutea') needles are an electric yellow throughout the season. Skyrocket juniper (*Juniperus scopulorum* 'Skyrocket') cools the color palette with tones of frosty blue. The Rohani copper beech (*Fagus sylvatica* 'Rohanii') is a stately tree with purple foliage.

above · Autumn can bring a whole new color palette into the garden. Remember to keep fall foliage in mind when coordinating with surrounding painted surfaces and blooming perennials.

right · A blue spruce provides a wonderful accent next to the soft gray-stained shingles of this house. This tree is salt-tolerant, so it is useful near sidewalks and roads.

facing page top · A well-pruned Japanese maple like this one is opened up to light and air and its horizontal structure emphasized. Always start by pruning out deadwood and vertical branches, then trim back overlapping branches.

facing page bottom · A theme and variation on yellow-gold is played out here with the new growth on these cedar trees and Japanese forest grasses (*Hakonechloa macra* 'Aureola') that surround a handsome stone bubbler.

A Cream and Lime Garden

One of our favorite clients asked us to create an abundant garden to complement her Swiss chalet–style home, which is set in a large grove of paper birches. We decided to make a garden based on creamy whites underplanted with perennials that feature chartreuse and lime-colored foliage. The result is a place that's straight out of a storybook!

right · The huge leaves of lime-colored plantain lily (*Hosta* 'Sum and Substance') bring a bold architecture to the corner of this stone-edged planter. The wrought-iron window cages that are planted with red begonias further set off the white stucco walls, overtopped with wooden sheathing.

below · Cream-colored peonies with yellow interior "eyes" (*Paeonia* 'Krinkled White') float above lady's mantle (*Alchemilla mollis*), whose blooms fall gracefully over the path into the garden. Creamy panicles of goatsbeard (*Aruncus dioicus*) float above it all.

Peonies and Gaura (*Gaura lindheimeri* 'Whirling Butterflies'), with its delicate, butterfly-shaped flowers, rise above the lady's mantle, reaching toward the sun.

FLOWERING TREES AND SHRUBS

Just as with trees, shrubs can be found in a variety of foliage hues. Even the color green has countless variations. Evergreen shrubs such as dwarf blue spruce (*Picea pungens* 'Glauca Globosa') and those with winter interest such as winterberry (*Ilex verticillata*) will provide color and structure to a garden even in the off-season months.

Many shrubs are bred for the splendor and color of their blooms. Some species have countless cultivars offering slight variations of color, height, flower size, hardiness, or bloom time. Generally speaking, flowering shrubs require much less maintenance than the average herbaceous perennial and are therefore a good way to get a display of flowers without the time commitment of a perennial garden.

Placing colorful shrubs in the perennial border can have a bold effect, so it is important to coordinate the flower and foliage colors of shrubs and perennials. For example, the purple hues of the leaves of the smoke bush (*Cotinus coggygria* 'Royal Purple') can be augmented by hints of purple in the garden such as purple-leaved Cimicifuga (*Actaea racemosa* 'Brunette') or snakeroot (*Eupatorium rugosum* 'Chocolate'). Ninebark (*Physocarpus opulifolius* 'Diablo') is the color of a deep red wine, which looks striking against a ground cover of chartreuse-leaved hostas or euphorbia.

above • Magenta blossoms cascade down a wall of glossy-leaved rhododendrons—a consistent favorite in temperate gardens.

left • Purple smoke bush (*Cotinus coggygria* 'Royal Purple') is always entrancing to children. Its puffy cloud of blooms is as soft to the touch as it looks.

above • An old-fashioned white lilac provides structure and fragrance in this garden at the same time that the purple wisteria blooms.

right • Hydrangea cultivars are plentiful, offering a wide range of bloom times from spring until fall. Shown here, blue lacecap hydrangea (*H. macrophylla normalis*), Annabelle smooth hydrangea (*H. arborescens* 'Annabelle') behind, and Tardiva hydrangea (*H. paniculata* 'Tardiva') in the background. You can ensure that your blue hydrangea (*H. macrophylla normalis*, blue lacecap, shown here) stays blue by feeding with aluminum sulfate.

Climbers

Climbers rise skyward out of the cluttered zone of plant competition. They require support, which can be informal as in the case of a tree or telephone pole, or formal, as with an arbor or pergola.

Different types of climbers have varying inclinations and growth habits. Some climbers, like roses and grapevines, have woody stems that remain year-round, even in the winter. Others, like some types of clematis, produce new growth from the ground each year and have a season of dormancy during which they might not be visible—or could be an unsightly tangle of bare vines. Be sure to choose carefully which type of climber you place at your front entry to avoid an unsightly mess in the off-season.

Vines climb in a variety of ways. Twining vines like wisteria send out shoots that encircle a support. Grapes and sweet peas twist their delicate tendrils around nearby supports to keep climbing. Other plants, like climbing roses, use their thorns to hold onto a support, while plants like ivy employ little rootlets to cling to the side of a house. Learning the growth habits of your climbing vines helps you to know best how to encourage them to wind their way up toward the sky.

top right · A blank wall is made interesting with a simple frame of cable on which creeping fig (*Ficus pumila*) climbs. Its small evergreen leaves happily cling to almost any surface in tropical homes and gardens.

bottom right · Clematis come in many colors and bloom times. This delicate blue variety (*Clematis* 'Blue Horizon') looks perfect against the burgundy tones of a bronze New Zealand flax plant (*Phormium* 'Dark Delight').

The vigorous trumpet vine (*Campsis radicans*) winds its way up a brick chimney. Considered invasive in some areas, it needs to be aggressively pruned to keep it from taking over the garden.

Perennials

Perennials are the workhorses of the traditional flower garden. They can be divided into two categories: herbaceous perennials that have soft stems that die back to the ground every year and nonherbaceous perennials that are evergreen, keeping their leaves throughout the seasons. Phlox, Shasta daisies, bee balm, and irises are all types of herbaceous perennials. Offering changing seasons of bloom and form, they constantly transform your garden landscape throughout the growing season. Their ability to survive the winter in dormancy is what distinguishes them from annuals.

Perennials are perhaps the trickiest plants with which to work in the garden. Gardeners should become familiar with the plants' height, color, shape, habit, season of bloom, and short- and long-term maintenance. A successful garden blends and balances the varied look and temperaments of multiple plants into a working composition. If you're a beginner, don't be intimidated: Gardeners old and new balance experience with trial and error. A perennial bed is always evolving.

top right • One of the great blue perennials for a garden is sea holly (*Eryngium x zabelli* 'Big Blue'), which thrives in hot, dry gardens. Here, its thistlelike flowers provide a delicate contrast with the pink perennial geranium flowers and the clipped boxwood globe, and against the neat leaves of baptisia in the background.

bottom right • Scarlet bee balm (*Monarda didyma*) stands tall by the side of white spires of tall fleece flower (*Persicaria polymorpha*) and mounds of stonecrop (*Sedum* sp.), all surrounding a birdbath filled with succulents.

facing page bottom • This complex multileveled garden shows good understanding of plant height and habit. The back of the border features taller screening shrubs, a privet hedge trimmed to 6 to 7 feet tall, the middle showcases larger perennials and lower shrubs in the 3- to 6-feet range, and planted at the front of the border are smaller annuals and perennials.

MEET YOUR NEIGHBORS

Every garden, large or small, can provide habitat for some of the world's creatures. Get to know the flora and fauna that are native to where you live and try to incorporate them into your garden design whenever possible. The beautiful flowers of the butterfly bush (*Buddleia*) are well known to attract butterflies—but many people don't realize that they do not provide any food for the insects' larvae. For many ornamental garden plants, there are attractive native plant alternatives that will provide food and habitat. Native bee balm (*Monarda* sp.), shown here, is a source of nectar for butterflies. Insects not only help to pollinate our flowers and fruit—they are also an irreplaceable food source for songbirds and other creatures.

Grasses, Sedges, and Rushes

Grasses are low-maintenance plants that work well in natural landscapes. Filling large spaces and small, there are ornamental grasses appropriate for a wide variety of landscape settings in a subtle range of color options. Sedge (*Carex*) varieties tend to be shade-tolerant, moisture-loving, and under 24 inches in height. Several species of *Miscanthus*, however, can reach over 10 feet tall and are happiest in low-nutrient soils in full sun.

above · Grasses also blossom, but in their case the flowers are referred to as inflorescences. Blue oat grass (*Helictotrichon sempervirens*) forms silvery-green clumps from which soft arching panicles appear in mid-to-late summer.

top right · Maiden grass (*Miscanthus sinensis* 'Morning Light') is a deer-resistant, drought-tolerant grass that looks good on its own or in groupings. Cut it back before or after snow falls and it will grow back to its former height by early summer.

bottom right · Cape rush is a grasslike evergreen perennial. Deer and rabbit resistant, it grows happily in a variety of soil, and like most grasses, loves the sun.

The chrome yellow of cushion spurge (*Euphorbia polychroma*) and the yellow-green needles of a cypress hedge (*Chamaecyparis pisifera* 'Filifera') surround the delicate purple inflorescence of switchgrass.

A Grassy Xeriscape

Xeriscaping (from the Greek word *xeros*, meaning "dry") means landscaping so that little or no supplemental water is needed to sustain plants' long-term growth. As its popularity grows in areas where drought is an annual occurrence, people are also coming to appreciate xeriscaping for the diverse beauty of the plantings and its reduced maintenance requirements.

This beautiful garden was designed by Rob DeGros for a homeowner in Saanich, British Columbia, who wanted an ecologically responsible, low-water, wildlife-friendly garden. Natural materials, like tree trunks, stumps, and local stones, were placed as subtle focal points around the garden. Grasses are used in abundance: in large swaths, as accents, knitting together perennials, shrubs, and trees, and as hedges and borders. The result is a landscape as subtle in coloration as it is soft in texture. The narrow, meandering gravel paths crunch underfoot as the visitor delights in exploring this gauzy, cloudlike world of beautiful plantings.

right · Under the deodar cedar, a gravel path winds through grasslands of fescues, panicums, and lavenders—about to flower.

facing page top · Stone steps beckon us upward, where the blue-needled bows of weeping blue Atlas cedar arch downward toward soft purple English lavender (*Lavendula angustifolia*) at its base. Across the path, the variegated foliage of blue bearded iris gesture upward, with heather at its feet.

facing page bottom · Xeriscaping need not rely upon cacti and succulents. Here, a mix of perennials and grasses, including blue oat grass, red hot poker, French and English lavender, and tall, blooming lamb's ear, makes the garden look invitingly wild, yet serene.

Ground Covers

Bare ground is difficult to maintain and has no real ecological benefits. Ground covers are earth carpets that provide weed protection, prevent surface run-off, diversify habitats, and enhance the beauty of the groundscape.

Contemporary gardeners are leaning away from ground covers like lawn grass that require a high degree of maintenance and lots of fertilizer and water to sustain. Instead, ground covers can act like a living mulch that can help retain moisture and eliminate the need for weeding. They are an effective way to add large swaths of color, texture, interest, or unity to the garden setting.

above • Who doesn't long for a moss garden in their own backyard? This wonderful forested landscape looks completely natural, except for its perfection. Leaf litter contained by ledge becomes the garden path.

left • A hillside of periwinkle (*Vinca minor*) and colorful creeping phlox (*Phlox subulata*) creates a floral carpet in early spring.

facing page • The soft spikes of blue fescue meld beautifully with blue asters and a ground cover of lavender-blue thyme. The red glazed container provides the perfect complement nearby.

above · Succulents like the century plant (*Agave americana* 'Alba'), foxtail agave (*Agave attenuata*), and blue finger (*Senecio mandraliscae*) shown here can be beautifully diverse and ornamental in nature and are excellent choices for the garden. Their varied forms create a living tapestry.

right · Thyme is a versatile herb and ground cover that can act as a soft mat on the ground. When you step on it, a wonderful herby aroma is released.

facing page · This ingenious green roof design not only catches water to sustain a surface garden, but it also has an overflow that diverts water to a garden below.

Bulbs

For those of us who live in cold climates, nothing pleases us more than the sight of the shoots of spring bulbs as they start to poke up through the snow. Bulbs—short-stemmed plants that store their own food underground—are among the easiest and most colorful flowers to grow. Snowdrops, crocus, daffodils, hyacinths, and tulips all are planted in the fall before the ground freezes; summer flowering bulbs like anemones, begonias, canna, calla lilies, dahlias, gladiolus, and lilies can be stored in a dry, cool space through the winter and then planted in the spring after the danger of frost.

Bulbs can be naturalized in a large field, tucked into the midst of perennial plantings, made into a special bulb garden, or even grown in containers. Because they are so easy to plant and care for, and bring an exuberance and longevity to the garden, they are immensely satisfying to gardeners and those who view them alike.

above · Bulbs start and end the gardening season with gloriously colorful displays.

left · Tulips offer a vast array of colors, sizes, and shapes. A lily-shaped pink tulip with green throat named Virichic unfolds toward the sun, while narcissus, grape hyacinths, and more tulips bloom behind them.

facing page · White daffodils planted in drifts along a long drive will multiply over time. It's best to naturalize daffodils in areas where you won't need to mow until the foliage yellows in preparation for dormancy.

Annuals

Nothing packs a punch like annual flowers. Annuals, by definition, survive only one season and are often used to supplement and extend blooming times, fill holes created by ephemerals, conceal the dying foliage of bulbs, or simply bring new color to the landscape.

Many annuals grow an astonishing amount during their single season. A tiny angel's trumpet (*Datura inoxia*) purchased at the garden center in May might be 3 feet tall and 5 feet wide by August. Be sure to learn the eventual size and growth habits of the annuals you choose—and look for new and unusual varieties. It's fun and easy to experiment with plants that will last only a year. Just be sure to give them plenty of compost or fertilizer, and observe their sun and moisture requirements.

facing page left · The lime-green and maroon foliage of coleus brightens dark corners and adds a vast variety of leaf color, size, and texture to any garden. A member of the mint family, coleus melds well with perennial and container plantings.

facing page right · Golden poppies (*Eschscholzia californica*), ubiquitous in California and other western states, are perennials in their native regions but annuals in colder zones, where they are killed by frost. Other tender perennials that cold-climate gardeners can use as annuals include impatiens, begonias, and pelargoniums (commonly called geraniums).

right · Blush-pink poppies combine with blue bachelor buttons in this meadow landscape. You can sow a meadow on your property as well—including annual and perennial flower mixtures that are great for cutting.

below · A vegetable garden with an unusual lavender-colored fence features a row of annual sage (*Salvia x sylvestris* 'May Night')—beloved for adding blue, red, or white flowers into any garden. Butterflies and hummingbirds feed on their nectar-rich blossoms.

Containers

As architectural accents in the garden, planted containers lend focal interest to the garden setting. Pots also keep planting soil off patios and decks while featuring bright-colored annuals or specimen plants. For cold-climate gardeners, containers are an excellent home for citrus trees and other exotics that look lovely on a terrace in summer but need to come indoors for the winter.

These days, containers come in a variety of materials and finishes. Traditional clay, light resin, stone, metal, or concrete pots bring a vast range of styles, colors, and textures to our gardens.

above • Annuals add a wealth of color to seasonal containers. Coordinate your colors with the colors of the garden. On this garden terrace, petunias and other vivid flowering annuals cascade over their vessel, visually blending with the gardens below.

below • The soft green-blue of kalanchoe leaves look cool within white pots on this tropical veranda.

above • Succulents perch elegantly in beautiful silver containers. The narrow tall pot features bold *Aeonium* rosettes; the round squat container holds peach-tipped aloe plants with swords of thick, fleshy leaves that are used to help heal wounds.

above · You can grow just about anything you want in a container. Here, several clay pots contain strawberries, herbs, and flowering perennials, set out on a peastone terrace that allows for ease of watering and drainage.

top left · The tiny sapphire flowers of lobelia spill down the side of this handsome container, which is filled with chartreuse potato vine (*Ipomoea* sp.) and overtopped by red begonias.

bottom left · Annual blue sage (*Salvia guaranitica* 'Black and Blue') complements the lime-yellow of the pennisetum grass in this pair of modern planters—a simple way to bring the garden closer.

An Abundant Garden

Whether you buy new containers, reuse a barrel or a tray, or make your own, potted plants—alone or in groupings—are a wonderful way to bring plants into every corner of your life. Author and garden expert Rob Proctor did just that—he created a fantastical container garden on a sunken terrace on his half-acre property in Denver. With so many pots in one place, each planted with a different plant species, you can't really tell where the containers stop and the in-the-ground plantings begin.

right • Teak benches form a harbor around sapphire blue Chinese ceramic stools, providing an enduring structure against which containers full of plantings are arrayed. The tall red-stemmed banana plant (*Musa* sp.) against the brick wall provides some vertical structure between the windows.

below • A tabby cat gazes out from beneath a spray of pale blue lobelia, doubtless disgruntled at the absence of catnip and catmint (*Nepeta* spp.) in her garden.

above · An earlier version of this terrace used a more muted palette of colors, on the seat cushions, the Chinese stools, and in the containers themselves. Container gardeners get to change out their pots every year, depending upon their mood.

left · The owner has created a cottage garden of colorful containers that mound up the steps to the dining room. You can combine colors in any way you want when you create such a delightful cacophony of hues, textures, and blooms.

Edibles

For reasons as diverse as thrift, taste, and ecology, more and more people are learning to grow food in their own backyard. Known to some as modern homesteading, this gardening tradition is reshaping the way we live and interact with our own landscapes. For some this may mean a few tomato plants in a pot on a patio. Others may indulge in a 1-acre vegetable plot and a flock of free-range chickens. Whatever the level and motivation, people are finding the edible garden to be one of the most satisfying ways to spend time on their land.

above • Why not grow a citrus tree on your front-entry deck? There you can pluck at will and, in warm climates, overwinter it in place.

facing page bottom • Horse troughs provide lots of space for vegetables when you only have a small space in the sun. Their handsome lozenge shape is raised 15 inches off the ground and makes for easy care and good drainage.

right • A walled garden enjoys raised beds of thick lumber and wood obelisks known as *tuteurs* in French. These handsome vertical focal points provide the perfect structure for growing climbing plants or vines, such as sweet peas or beans.

below • The edible garden can have a beautiful and organized, yet informal, charm. Here, a berry house formed from rustic logs and netting keeps critters and birds out so that the owner can get to the harvest first.

DETAILS

Crafting the details of your landscape

IN THE

links inside to outside and brings focus to the whole property.

LANDSCAPE

Delighting in the Details

Look around your house—what is it that most catches your eye? Often it's the little details—the pictures on the wall, the accent colors on the pillows, the hanging chandelier, the favorite vase filled with flowers—that enliven and personalize a space and bring aesthetic delight to you and your friends and family. Similarly, it's the details you place outside that add a layer of finish and sparkle to the landscape around your house. Selecting and placing appropriate focal points—including fire and water elements—ornament, and lighting all enhance our enjoyment of home outside.

The special decorative objects that add an embellishing note to our homes enhance our enjoyment of our property. Some of us prefer choosing one-of-a-kind pieces that stand alone in the landscape; others enjoy making and displaying collections and placing them in just the right places. Just as we decorate the inside of our homes with special knickknacks, favorite collections, or seasonal ornaments, so too can we adorn our landscapes with beloved objects—the details that catch the eye and make us smile.

top right · With thick epiphytic roots absorbing moisture from the air, an orchid simply tied to a tree branch will thrive in humid climes and delight the eye with its intricate beauty.

bottom right · A massive millwheel found a second life as a breakfast table in this Vermont garden. Chives, sage, thyme, and tarragon grow happily from the center opening where the wooden axle would have been.

Even a blue-painted girl's bike can become a focal point in a garden. A flowerpot rests where the seat should have been, and several stalks of blue bearded iris grow high around the blue violas (*Viola cornuta* 'Perfection Blue') in a clay pot in the basket.

Frames

A frame around a painting creates a clear border that surrounds and highlights the image within. Similarly, each window in our house can act as a frame that makes a picture out of the landscape in our view. We can also use elements of architecture, like porch posts or gateways, to define the edges of a scene and thereby draw the eye. Or the space between two tree trunks forms a natural frame around the setting sun at dusk. When we find or create a frame around a focal object— by placing a pedestal beneath a sculpture, a moongate that frames a specimen tree, or a pergola that frames the clouds in the sky—we transform our normal view of the landscape around us and make it special.

above · The structure of this rustic front porch is made of tree trunks. A single Adirondack chair gazes out between the posts, which frame a gnarly tree—the focus of the garden.

left · Climbing hydrangea and wisteria vines twist and turn up the posts of this garden arbor that houses a stone pathway set amongst hosta plantings and frames a view of a container beyond.

facing page · A natural frame of living birch trunks, their canopy, and grasses at their base provides an oblique view into the swimming pool terrace and its comfortable weathered teak chairs.

Focal Points

When a landscape is designed around a focal point, it tends to draw us in and hold our attention. Focal points are the objects in a landscape that catch our eyes, like a central sculpture, a distant view, or a bubbling fountain. Focal points may be tiny or over-scale, viewed close-up or in the distance, in motion or not. A well-placed focal point can be the center-piece of a whole landscape.

Focal points in the landscape catch the eye when forces of nature animate them. The sparkle of flowing water, the movement of wind chimes, the flitting of birds at a feeder are just a few of the many ways that actual movement brings focal objects to life. Another way is to find or create sculptures that feel as though they're in motion and place them in your garden.

facing page top · A concrete Buddha meditates quietly on a wooden platform in a verdant garden. We follow his gaze downward to someone's beloved collection of stones, including one with a perfect heart shape.

facing page bottom left · A metal armillary sphere was an early astronomical model of the celestial globe used to teach astronomy, make geometric calculations, and understand the location of the heavenly bodies at different times of the year. The arrow is meant to be adjustable to the local latitude.

facing page bottom right · A number of elements contribute to the framing effect in this design: the neatly trimmed hedges approaching the bench, the round potted boxwoods flanking it (and echoing the shape of the ornamental ball), and the rose-decked arching trellis overhead. In a playful twist reminiscent of a Dutch painting, a framed mirror reflects it all back to the viewer.

right · Festive metal stake lights with candles light up steps through a beautiful tropical garden. Once you've dealt with the big moves, it's often the little things that bring ambience and romantic delight to our gardens.

The owner of this beautiful garden loved the formality of clipped hedges combined with the romance of flowers. Metal vases flank the central bed, where hollyhocks and blue delphiniums rise high above hydrangea, dahlias, and snapdragons.

STONE

Used correctly, stones can act as both focal point and backbone of any landscape. They appear more natural when they seem to emerge from deep within the ground and are set into odd pairings or sets of threes, fives, and sevens. While stones set vertically more easily grab our attention, those that are set parallel and low to the ground feel restful, as though they've always been there.

right • Rock cap moss grows in the cleft of this vertical stone, while lichens dot its surface like skin. When you're using stone in the landscape, make sure that it is well weathered by the elements so that it looks like it's always been there.

below • Whenever possible, use local stone. Not only is it more affordable and readily available, it will also look most natural in a designed landscape.

Before you try to set stones in a landscape, seek out natural ponds and streams to learn what nature does. Boulders should feel as though they are emerging from the earth and should be set so you can't see under them.

WATER

Water provides one of the best points of focus in a landscape. Moving water draws both our eyes and ears, and often birds and other critters as well. Elaborate waterfalls and decorative backyard streams may be more than many of us have the means to create, but simple all-in-one garden fountains can add visual and aural delights on a shoestring budget.

Still water also delights the eye while cooling the atmosphere. Small lily ponds or simple birdbaths can reflect the movement in the sky and bring contemplative delight into the backyard landscape.

above • A downspout pours into the beach stone dry well, right into the soil below. This way, it can water the nearby plants and replenish the aquifer, deep below the surface.

right • A long, narrow bluestone rill bubbles through a capstone. It provides a solid back to an outdoor couch and a border to the garden beyond. The sound of water entices the family outside and invites children to play in this open-air room.

A stone dunking pool lets swimmers rinse the salt off on their way to the changing room. There is something deeply satisfying about being able to see from one body of water to another: water to water.

above · A newly carved millstone continues the theme of circles in the landscape. Behind it rests a hot tub, so its owners get the delight of sitting within water while looking over bubbling water to a long view of mountains beyond.

left · Nestled into a garden of Pride of Madeira (*Echium candicans*), salvia, and aloe, this glazed pot is a cooling oasis in a dry garden. With a simple bubbler and recirculating fountain pump, its catch basin covered by river stones at the base, this fountain uses minimal water for a big impact.

facing page · A Japanese-style garden built into a hillside is focused around a small wooden viewing pavilion and a simple stone water basin that is filled through a bamboo pipe. Water flows over the sides into the peastone drain at its feet.

A Swimming Pond

This lovely Vermont pond was renovated by a local landscape contractor, but it didn't meet the needs of its owners. They asked JMMDS to make it work better both as a swimming pond and as a focal element in their pastoral landscape. We began by carving out an entry area with existing stones, adding some soft hills, and sculpting harbors and promontories. We then planted native trees, shrubs, and perennials that melded in with the beautiful surrounding hills and knitted it all together with grassy paths around the perimeter. The result works well for our client, who loves jumping off the long diving stone for a cool swim in the pond, sitting on the little bench and terrace by its entrance, harvesting blueberries as they become ripe, and picking flowers to fill her vases in the charming updated farmhouse.

We designed the stones so that they not only framed the entry point to the pond, but also protruded into it to allow for diving. Balancing boulders so that they feel as though they've always been there is one of the great delights of stone setting.

left · We created a grass path around the pond so that its owners can enjoy reflections of their updated farmhouse at the end of a summer's day.

bottom left · When you have a large focal point like a pond, you need good-sized plantings to bring it into scale. Here, large swaths of pink queen-of-the-prairie (*Filipendula rubra* 'Venusta') bloom in the distance, while bright red daylilies (*Hemerocallis* 'Pardon Me') and heather spikes (*Agastache* 'Blue Fortune') bring a riot of color to the foreground.

bottom right · A flat fieldstone terrace provides a clear entry point to the swimming pond.

FIRE

From time immemorial, fire has been a vital part of our outdoor landscapes. Originally used primarily for cooking and warmth, fire has increasingly become an ornamental and focal feature that draws families and friends into the landscape at night. Fire pits, fire bowls, fireplaces, bread and pizza ovens, and outdoor kitchens and grills—whether wood- or gas-fired—all animate and bring thermal delight to our experience of the out-of-doors.

right • An inset gas fireplace unit is not only easy to turn on and off, but it also extends the usability of this outdoor room into the colder seasons, while providing a marvelous thermal counterpoint to the body of water beyond.

below • A concrete fire pit sits cleanly on a mahogany deck surrounded by verdant lawn. The concrete porch and paving stones set in grass complement the choice of materials.

This outdoor fire pit has a built-up back that holds the heat and protects the fire from drafts. The large stone in front of it acts as both bench and table for perching drinks glasses or holding the fixings for s'mores.

Fire and Water

Designer Ron Rule created a small urban garden in Vancouver, British Columbia, that includes an outdoor fireplace, a built-in barbecue, and a sculptural water wall out of concrete and stone to mask the noise of street traffic. Inset charcoal paving stones highlight seating areas, much like an outdoor carpet, in both the outdoor dining and living rooms. No lawn is present here—just lush plantings along with the sounds of a crackling fire and splashing water.

Outdoor fireplaces can be freestanding or built into the wall of a structure. If installing a new outdoor fireplace area, be sure to hire a licensed contractor who will observe all safety precautions. Don't forget to consider convenient (and attractive) wood storage and ash removal in your design.

right · A concrete water wall fountain measures 8 feet tall by 12 feet long and 2 feet deep and is encrusted with small oblong stone tiles to match the charcoal pavers.

below · This outdoor living room can be used throughout the year in temperate Vancouver. A verdant pillar marks the level change between dining and living areas, and plantings soften the concrete retaining walls throughout.

above • This stainless steel grill was built into a chimney adjacent to the dining area, making it easy for the cook to bring hot food to the table without burning the house down.

OUTDOOR KITCHENS

Many of us are able to locate open-air dining spaces right next to our kitchens so that carrying food between inside and out is not an impediment to eating under the stars. These days, durable, moveable grills, with extension arms that carry platters and grilling utensils, can be used no matter the season.

Others prefer the convenience of an outdoor kitchen, complete with built-in grill, refrigerator, and even a prep sink. Because they necessitate the building of walls to house the different elements, it pays to use the services of a landscape or kitchen professional to integrate the kitchen into a full-scale landscape design. Where you locate the kitchen—whether in the middle of the entertainment space or to the edge—will depend upon the personality of the chef.

above • Some people prefer to place their grill where no one can see it, in this case screened by a pool house. Note how all the wooden elements match: decking, fencing, and cladding.

above • This outdoor kitchen truly feels like an extension of home. It also provides every amenity a chef could want, ensuring that no one will be stuck indoors cooking while everyone else is enjoying the party outside. A wide counter to the left of the built-in grill ensures plenty of room for the buffet.

Furniture

With so many outdoor furniture choices on the market these days, it's tempting to buy whatever's on sale at the time. But just like inside, finding the right armchair, table, or sofa can make or break the look and feel of an open-air room. Consider harmonizing the furniture's style with that of your house and using color to match or accent the plantings around it.

top right • It's fun to pick furniture and cushions that support your garden's theme. Here, white canvas pillows underscore the white garden while contrasting beautifully with the bright hues of the hanging baskets above.

bottom right • Both the hammock that swings between two huge trees and the two chaise longues that flank a rill remind us of the delight of lying down under the stars, either alone or as an intimate duo.

below • A slab of wood resting on two round stones is all you need to enable your visitors to enjoy your garden path. Make sure you back up your bench with plantings and that there's something interesting to look at in the viewshed.

right • A glass tabletop is an excellent way to provide a large surface for accommodating many guests without dominating or overwhelming the space. The understated table allows the bright, fun chairs to steal the show.

below • A little white pool house, complete with comfortable couch and privacy curtains, beckons, all set within a fragrant lavender garden. Each piece of furniture here is thoughtfully curated by the owner to bring comfort—and style—to this beautiful pool garden.

above • This designer drew a simple line—in this case, a wooden bench—that divides landscape from architecture. The space between becomes an expansive outdoor room, both under the eaves and out from them.

above • A teak dining set perfectly suits the colors of the stone terrace and natural ledge. Right outside the kitchen, it's located for ease of access with maximal privacy.

A crunchy peastone terrace is set off from its neighbors by an inexpensive stockade fence. A hedge separates dining area from living area. The owner invested wisely in good dining furniture: charming bistro chairs, wicker armchairs, and a long wooden table that can seat a crowd.

Lighting

Thoughtful outdoor lighting puts the frosting on the cake. It can not only highlight and enhance views of your garden from indoors at night, but it can also extend the hours during which you enjoy your outdoor spaces. You don't need to light the entire landscape; look for the particular features you wish to illuminate. Use lighting as a safety feature, making paths and steps clearly visible at night, and make it easy for you and your guests to travel between outdoor living spaces and the house itself. Look for solar and alternative-powered options that will reduce your energy usage; in recent years, LEDs have improved greatly, now offering warmer light and dimming options that beautify the nighttime landscape.

right • Find lighting fixtures that blend with or complement the style of your home—perhaps echoing the pattern of an architectural feature such as a front-door design or leaded-glass window.

Café lights strung from house to tree light up the fire pit area at this wonderful family home.

above · A variety of light sources playfully illuminate this outdoor living space, from the golden light filtered through the poolhouse glass to the functional-yet-beautiful stairway fixtures to the magical underwater lighting in the pool and hot tub.

left · Uplighting from either a can set into the ground or a moveable hooded element can spotlight a special tree, feature, or path. The chandelier set under the porch casts plenty of light on this garden entry.

Party Central

This three-level outdoor space in a close-knit neighborhood fulfills many functions in a small area. Sitting and entertaining, outdoor dining for children and adults, and a private entry from a shared driveway all knit fluidly together.

The client asked Vermont landscape designer George Zavis of Sight Design to help them create a fun family entertainment space. First, in order to maintain existing views but also gain some privacy, he created a sunken outdoor living room, complete with rustic fireplace. To screen the shared driveway from view, he erected a fence and built an indirect path from driveway to back door. He selected local stone for walls and steps, bluestone for walkways, and peastone for the sunken terrace. He then planted trees, hedges, and perennials to soften the whole. Now people gather throughout the space. With as many as 43 guests there at once, it's Party Central!

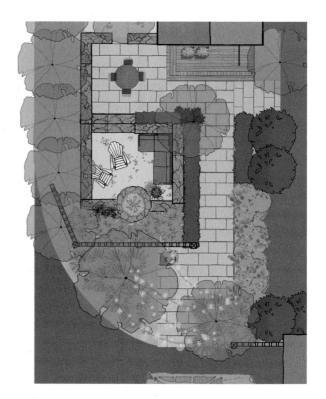

left · A sculpturally pruned specimen tree and a line of billowing catmint point the way to the front door—but the string of dancing lights overhead signals that you might get sidetracked into some fun along the way.

above · A restrained palette of plantings in various shades of green feels restful—and allows the lime and purple dining set on the terrace to pop!

right · The outdoor living area is a cozy harbor, backed on one side by a neat hedge and on the other by a wall of graduated textures: stone, feathery plantings, wooden latticework, and tree branches dotted with fairy lights. With a glowing fire and a starry sky above, the space epitomizes the magic of summer nights.

CREDITS

p. i: © Allan Mandell, design: Linda Ernst, Portland, OR

p. ii: © Susan Teare, design: JMMDS

p. iv (left to right): © Home Outside Inc., design: Home Outside; © Randy O'Rourke, design: Nancy McCabe Garden Designs, Falls Village, CT; © Susan Teare, design: JMMDS; © Tria Giovan

p. v (left to right): © Randy O'Rourke; © Allan Mandell, design: Lily Maxwell, Victoria, BC; © Lee Anne White, design: Simmonds & Associates; © Tria Giovan

p. 2 (top, left to right): © Mark Lohman, design: Janet Lohman Design; © Carolyn L. Bates Photography, design: Cynthia Knauf; © Melissa Clark Photography, design: Everett Garden Designs; © Tria Giovan

(bottom): © Brian Vanden Brink, design: Hutker Architects, Horiuchi & Solien Landscape Architects

p. 3: © Lee Anne White, design: Jeni Webber, Landscape Architect

CHAPTER 1

p. 4: © Mark Lohman, design: Janet Lohman Design

p. 6: (top) © Randy O'Rourke; (bottom) © Brian Vanden Brink, design: South Mountain Company

p. 7: © Allan Mandell, design: Paul Murphy, Victoria, BC

p. 8: (top) © Randy O'Rourke, design: Nancy McCabe Garden Designs, Falls Village, CT; (bottom) © Laurie Black, design: Lisa Port, APLD, Banyon Tree Design Studio

p. 10: (top) © Susan Teare, design: JMMDS; © Randy O'Rourke

p. 11: © Randy O'Rourke

pp. 12-13: © Susan Teare, design: JMMDS

p. 14: (top) © Brian Vanden Brink, design: Carl Solander Architect; (bottom) © Susan Teare, design: John K Szczepaniak, Landscape Architect

p. 15: © Lee Anne White, design: Jeni Webber, Landscape Architect

p. 16: (top) © Brian Vanden Brink, design: Scott Simons, Architect; (bottom) © Brian Vanden Brink

p. 17: © Home Outside Inc., design: Home Outside

p. 18: (top) © Tria Giovan; (bottom) © Brian Vanden Brink

p. 19: © (bottom) © Brian Vanden Brink, design: Weatherend Estate Furniture

CHAPTER 2

p. 20: © Ken Gutmaker, design: Brooks Kolb LLC, Landscape Architecture

p. 22: (top) © Tria Giovan; (bottom) © Tria Giovan

p. 24: (top) © Home Outside Inc., design: Home Outside; (bottom) © Ken Gutmaker, design: Nancy Harrington, Evergreen Garden Design

p. 25: (top) © Tria Giovan; (bottom) © Randy O'Rourke, design: Nancy McCabe Garden Designs, Falls Village, CT

pp. 26-27: © Susan Teare, design: JMMDS

p. 28: (top) © Randy O'Rourke; (bottom) © Ken Gutmaker, design: Lisa Port, APLD, Banyon Tree Design Studio

p. 29: © Susan Teare, design: JMMDS

p. 30: (top) © Laurie Black, design: Lisa Port, APLD, Banyon Tree Design Studio; (bottom) © Tria Giovan

p. 31: © Mark Lohman, design: Janet Lohman Design

p. 32: (top) © Tria Giovan; (bottom) © Lee Anne White, design: Sean Weatherill, Weatherill & Associates

p. 33: © Tria Giovan

p. 34: © Lee Anne White, design: Simmonds & Associates

p. 35: (top) © Susan Teare, design: John K Szczepaniak, Landscape Architect; (bottom) © Lee Anne White, design: Jeni Webber, Landscape Architect

p. 36: (top) © Ken Gutmaker, design: Nancy Harrington, Evergreen Garden Design; (bottom) © Lee Anne White, design: Jeni Webber, Landscape Architect

p. 37: © Allan Mandell, design: Linda Ernst, Portland, OR

p. 38: (top) © Susan Teare, design: George Zavis, Sight Design; (bottom) © Mark Lohman, design: Greg Grisamore Landscape Design

p. 39: (top) © Susan Teare, design: George Zavis, Sight Design; (bottom) © Randy O'Rourke

p. 40: © Mark Lohman, design: Janet Lohman Design

p. 41: © Randy O'Rourke, design: Robert Hanss

p. 42: (top) © Randy O'Rourke; (bottom) © Ken Gutmaker, design: Lisa Port, APLD, Banyon Tree Design Studio

p. 43: © Randy O'Rourke

p. 44: (left) © Randy O'Rourke; (top right) © Lisa Port, design: Lisa Port, APLD, Banyon Tree Design Studio; (bottom right) © Lee Anne White, design: Simmonds & Associates

p. 45: © Brian Vanden Brink, design: Horiuchi & Solien Landscape Architects

p. 46: (top) © Brian Vanden Brink; (bottom) Grey Crawford, design: JMMDS

p. 47: (top) © Jim Fiora, design: Sandra Vlock of Arbonies King Vlock, Architects; (bottom) © Lee Anne White, design: Jeni Webber, Landscape Architect

pp. 48–49: (left) © Susan Teare, design: Maggie Judycki, GreenThemes Incorporated

p. 50: (top) © Randy O'Rourke, design: Nancy McCabe Garden Designs, Falls Village, CT; (bottom left) © Susan Teare, design: Maggie Judycki, GreenThemes Incorporated; (bottom right) © Susan Teare, design: John K Szczepaniak, Landscape Architect

p. 51: (left) © Mark Lohman, design: Greg Grisamore Landscape Design

p. 52–53: (left to right) © Susan Teare, design: JMMDS; © Randy O'Rourke, design: Tom & Linda Petrocine; © Christine Libon, design: John K Szczepaniak, Landscape Architect and Christine Libon, Horticulturist

CHAPTER 3

p. 54: © Brian Vanden Brink

p. 56: (top) © Tria Giovan; (bottom) © Melissa Clark Photography, design: Everett Garden Designs

p. 57: © Tria Giovan

p. 58: (top) © Tria Giovan; (bottom) © Susan Teare, design: John K Szczepaniak, Landscape Architect

p. 59: © Brian Vanden Brink

p. 60: (top) © Jim Fiora, design: Arbonies King Vlock, Architects;

(bottom) © Susan Teare, design: JMMDS

p. 61: © Randy O'Rourke

p. 62: (top) © Brian Vanden Brink, design: Horiuchi & Solien Landscape Architects, Adolfo Perez, Architect; (bottom) © Susan Teare, design: JMMDS

p. 63: (top) © Lisa Port, design: Lisa Port, APLD, Banyon Tree Design Studio; (bottom) © Randy O'Rourke

pp. 64–65: © Susan Teare, design: John K Szczepaniak, Landscape Architect

p. 66: (top) © Randy O'Rourke; (bottom) © Randy O'Rourke

p. 67: © Tria Giovan

p. 68: (top) © Chipper Hatter, materials: Amcor; (bottom) © Susan Teare, design: John K Szczepaniak, Landscape Architect

p. 69: (top, left to right) © Lee Anne White, design: Jeni Webber, Landscape Architect; © Ken Gutmaker, design: Lisa Port, APLD, Banyon Tree Design Studio; © Lee Anne White, design: Sean Weatherill, Weatherill & Associates; (bottom, left to right) © Randy O'Rourke; © Randy O'Rourke; © Allan Mandell, design: Graham Smyth, Victoria, BC

pp. 70–71: © Susan Teare, design: John K Szczepaniak, Landscape Architect

p. 72: (left) © Paul Willard, Paul Willard Photography, design: Everett Garden Designs; (top right) © Lee Anne White, design: Simmonds & Associates; (bottom right) © Lee Anne White, design: Jeni Webber, Landscape Architect

p. 73: © Tria Giovan

p. 74: (top) © Tria Giovan; (bottom) © Lee Anne White, design: Simmonds & Associates

p. 75: (top) © Susan Teare, design: JMMDS; (bottom) © Tria Giovan

p. 76: (left) © Brian Vanden Brink, design: Hutker Architects; (top right) © Susan Teare, design: JMMDS; (bottom right) © Susan Teare, design: JMMDS

p. 77: (top left) © Tria Giovan; (bottom left) © Brian Vanden Brink, design: Hutker Architects; (bottom right) © Susan Teare, design: JMMDS

p. 78: (left) © Tria Giovan; (top

right) © Mark Lohman, design: Janet Lohman Design; (bottom right) © Carolyn L. Bates Photography, design: Cynthia Knauf

p. 79: (top) © Tria Giovan; (bottom) © Randy O'Rourke

p. 80: (top) © Susan Teare, design: JMMDS; (bottom) © Randy O'Rourke

p. 81: © Mark Lohman, design: Mike Eagleton, Landscape Service & Design

p. 82: (top) © Tria Giovan; (bottom) © Brian Vanden Brink, design: Sam Williamson, Landscape Architect

p. 83: © Brian Vanden Brink, design: Payette Associates Architects

p. 84: (top) © Banyon Tree Design Studio, design: Lisa Port, APLD, Banyon Tree Design Studio; (bottom) © Ken Gutmaker, design: Patricia St. John, APLD, St. John Landscapes

p. 85: © Randy O'Rourke

pp. 86–87: © Ken Gutmaker, design: Lisa Port, APLD, Banyon Tree Design Studio

CHAPTER 4

p. 88: © Tria Giovan

p. 90: (top) © Lee Anne White, design: Jeni Webber, Landscape Architect; (bottom) © Tria Giovan

p. 91: © Susan Teare, design: JMMDS; (bottom) © Randy O'Rourke

p. 92: (top) © Tria Giovan; (bottom) © Brian Vanden Brink, design: Polhemus Savery DaSilva Architects, Builders

p. 93: (top) © Ken Gutmaker, design: Lisa Port, APLD, Banyon Tree Design Studio; (bottom) © Susan Teare, design: Maggie Judycki, GreenThemes Incorporated

p. 94: (top) © Susan Teare, design: JMMDS; (bottom) © Brian Vanden Brink, design: Horiuchi and Solien Landscape Architects

p. 95: (top) © Susan Teare, design: JMMDS; (bottom) © Tria Giovan

p. 96: (top) © Tria Giovan; (bottom) © Lee Anne White, design: Sean Weatherill, Weatherill & Associates

p. 97: © Susan Teare, design: Maggie Judycki, GreenThemes Incorporated

p. 98: (top) © Randy O'Rourke; (bottom) © Lee Anne White, design: Sean Weatherill, Weatherill & Associates

p. 99: (top left) © Chipper Hatter, materials: Georgia Masonry Supply; (top right) © Randy O'Rourke; (bottom left) © Tria Giovan; (bottom right) © Tria Giovan

p. 100: (left) © Lee Anne White, design: Simmonds & Associates; (right) © Ken Gutmaker, design: Lisa Port, APLD, Banyon Tree Design Studio

p. 101: (top) © Lee Anne White, design: Sean Weatherill, Weatherill & Associates; (bottom) © Susan Teare, design: JMMDS

p. 102: (top) © Melissa Clark Photography, design: Everett Garden Designs; (bottom) © Tria Giovan

p. 103: (top) © Susan Teare, design: Maggie Judycki, GreenThemes Incorporated; (bottom) © Lee Anne White, design: Sean Weatherill, Weatherill & Associates

pp. 104–105: © MJ McCabe, design: MJ McCabe–Garden Design

p. 106: (top) © Randy O'Rourke; (bottom) © Tria Giovan

p. 107: (top) © Allan Mandell, design: Graham Smyth, Victoria, BC; (bottom) © Janis Nicolay, design: Ron Rule Consultants Ltd.

p. 108: (top) © Lee Anne White, design: Jeni Webber, Landscape Architect; (bottom) © Susan Teare, design: JMMDS

p. 109: (top left) © Randy O'Rourke, design: Nancy McCabe Garden Designs, Falls Village, CT; (top right) © Tria Giovan; (bottom © Carolyn L. Bates Photography, design: Cynthia Knauf

p. 110: (top) © Susan Teare, design: JMMDS; (bottom) © Lee Anne White, design: Sean Weatherill, Weatherill & Associates

p. 111: (top) © Lee Anne White, design: Sean Weatherill, Weatherill & Associates; (bottom) © Randy O'Rourke

p. 112: (left) © Ken Gutmaker, design: Patricia St. John, APLD, St. John Landscapes; (top right) © Susan Teare, design: JMMDS; (bottom right) © Randy O'Rourke

p. 113: © Allan Mandell, design: Graham Smyth, Victoria, BC

p. 114: (top) © Mark Lohman; (bottom) © Randy O'Rourke

p. 115: (left) © Mark Lohman, design:

Greg Grisamore Landscape Design; (top right) © Allan Mandell, design: Joan and Gary Cunningham, Victoria, BC; (bottom right) © Susan Teare, design: JMMDS

CHAPTER 5

p. 116: © Mark Lohman, design: Janet Lohman Design

p. 118: (top) © Claire Jones, design: Claire Jones Landscapes, LLC; (bottom) © Susan Teare, design: John K Szczepaniak, Landscape Architect

p. 119: © Tria Giovan

p. 120: (top) © Tria Giovan; (bottom) © Ken Gutmaker, design: Brooks Kolb LLC, Landscape Architecture

p. 121: © Mark Lohman, design: Janet Lohman Design

pp. 122–123: © Ken Gutmaker, design: Lisa Port, APLD, Banyon Tree Design Studio

p. 124: (left) © Randy O'Rourke; (top right) © Melissa Clark Photography, design: Everett Garden Designs; (bottom right) © MJ McCabe, design: MJ McCabe–Garden Design

p. 125: © Brian Vanden Brink, design: Horiuchi and Solien Landscape Architects

pp. 126–127: © Mark Lohman, design: Janet Lohman Design

p. 128: (left) © MJ McCabe, design: MJ McCabe–Garden Design; (top right) © Brian Vanden Brink, design: Hutker Architects, landscape design: Carlos Montoya; (bottom right) © Ken Gutmaker, design: Brooks Kolb LLC, Landscape Architecture

p. 129: (top) © Lee Anne White, design: Sean Weatherill, Weatherill & Associates; (bottom) © Bill Sumner Photography, design: JMMDS

p. 130: (left) © Allan Mandell, design: Stacie Crooks, Edmonds, WA; (right) © Mark Lohman, design: Rob Proctor Garden Design

p. 131: (top) © Allan Mandell, design: Rob DeGros, N. Saanich, BC; (bottom) © Lee Anne White, design: Jeni Webber, Landscape Architect

p. 132: (top) © Virginia Weiler, design: Nancy Spencer and Kevin Lindsey; (bottom) © Susan Teare, design: John K Szczepaniak, Landscape Architect

p. 133: (left) © Mark Lohman, design:

Janet Lohman Design; (top right) © Chipper Hatter, national hardscape manufacturer: Oldcastle APG; (bottom right) © Randy O'Rourke

p. 134: (left) © Janis Nicolay, design: Ron Rule Consultants Ltd.; (top right) © Randy O'Rourke; (bottom right) © Tria Giovan

p. 135: © Susan Teare, design: JMMDS

p. 136: (left) © Mark Lohman, design: Janet Lohman Design; (top right) © Susan Teare, design: John K Szczepaniak, Landscape Architect; (bottom right) © Randy O'Rourke

p. 137: © Randy O'Rourke

p. 138: (top) © Ken Gutmaker, design: Lisa Port, APLD, Banyon Tree Design Studio; (bottom) © Randy O'Rourke, design: Nancy McCabe Garden Designs, Falls Village, CT

p. 139: (top) © Chipper Hatter, landscape architect: Jeffrey Carbo, ASLA; (bottom) © Virginia Weiler, design: Nancy Spencer and Kevin Lindsey

CHAPTER 6

p. 140: © Susan Teare, design: JMMDS

p. 142: © Susan Teare, design: JMMDS; (bottom) © Ken Gutmaker, design: Lisa Port, APLD, Banyon Tree Design Studio

p. 143: © Susan Teare, design: JMMDS

p. 144: (top) © Lee Anne White, design: Simmonds & Associates; (bottom) © Randy O'Rourke, design: Nancy McCabe Garden Designs, Falls Village, CT

p. 145: © Susan Teare, design: JMMDS

pp. 146–147: © Ken Gutmaker, design: Nancy Harrington, Evergreen Garden Design

p. 148: © Allan Mandell, design: Joan and Gary Cunningham, N. Saanich, BC

p. 149: (top) © Melissa Clark Photography, design: Everett Garden Designs; (bottom) © Mark Lohman, design: Janet Lohman Design

p. 150: (top) © Susan Teare, design: John K Szczepaniak, Landscape Architect; (bottom) © Mark Lohman, design: Greg Grisamore Landscape Design

p. 151: © Tria Giovan

p. 152: (top) © Susan Teare, design: John K Szczepaniak, Landscape Architect; (bottom) © Mark Lohman, design: Janet Lohman Design

p. 153: (top) © Susan Teare, design: Maggie Judycki, GreenThemes Incorporated; (bottom) © Susan Teare, design: George Zavis, Sight Design

pp. 154–155: © Ken Gutmaker, design: Brooks Kolb LLC, Landscape Architecture

p. 156: (top) © Brooks Kolb, design: Brooks Kolb LLC, Landscape Architecture; (bottom) © Ken Gutmaker, design: Lisa Port, APLD, Banyon Tree Design Studio

p. 157: (top) © Jim Westphalen Photography, design: Cynthia Knauf; (bottom) © Randy O'Rourke

pp. 158–159: © Susan Teare, design: JMMDS

p. 160: (left) © Lee Anne White, design: Jeni Webber, Landscape Architect; (right) © Allan Mandell, design: Elizabeth Chatfield, Victoria, BC

p. 161: (top) © Allan Mandell, design: Elizabeth Chatfield, Victoria, BC; (bottom) © Susan Teare, design: JMMDS

p. 162: (top) © Tria Giovan; (bottom) © MJ McCabe, design: MJ McCabe–Garden Design

p. 163: © Melissa Clark Photography, design: Everett Garden Designs

p. 164: (top) © Allan Mandell, design: Lily Maxwell, Victoria, BC; (bottom) © Melissa Clark Photography, design: Everett Garden Designs

p. 165: (top) © Susan Teare; (bottom) © Randy O'Rourke

p. 166: (left) © Allan Mandell, design: Rob DeGros, N. Saanich, BC; (top right) © Roy Grogan, design: John K Szczepaniak, Landscape Architect; (bottom right) © Ken Gutmaker, design: Nancy Harrington, Evergreen Garden Design

p. 167: © Allan Mandell, design: Lily Maxwell, Victoria, BC

pp. 168-169: © Allan Mandell, design: Rob DeGros, N. Saanich, BC

p. 170: (top) © Randy O'Rourke; (bottom) © Randy O'Rourke

p. 171: © Lee Anne White, design: Jeni Webber, Landscape Architect

p. 172: © Susan Teare, design: Cynthia Knauf

p. 173: (top) © Mark Lohman, design: Janet Lohman Design; (bottom) © Claire Jones, design: Claire Jones Landscapes, LLC

p. 174: (left and right) © MJ McCabe, design: MJ McCabe–Garden Design;

p. 175: © Tria Giovan

p. 176: (left) © Allan Mandell, design: Linda Ernst, Portland, OR; (right) © Brian Vanden Brink

p. 177: (top) © Susan Teare, design: JMMDS; (bottom) © Randy O'Rourke, design: Nancy McCabe Garden Designs, Falls Village, CT

p. 178: (left) © Susan Teare, design: JMMDS; (top right) © Susan Teare, design: JMMDS; (bottom right) © Lee Anne White, design: Sean Weatherill, Weatherill & Associates

p. 179: (top left) © Susan Teare; (bottom left) © Susan Teare, design: George Zavis, Sight Design; (right) © Mark Lohman, design: Janet Lohman Design

pp. 180–181: © Mark Lohman, design: Rob Proctor Garden Design

p. 182: (top) © Mark Lohman, design: Janet Lohman Design; (bottom) © Lisa Port, design: Lisa Port, APLD, Banyon Tree Design Studio

p. 183: (top) © Tria Giovan; (bottom) © Elizabeth Halley, design: Elizabeth Halley Landscape Design

CHAPTER 7

p. 184: © Allan Mandell, design: Wendy Pickin, Sidney, BC

p. 186: (top) © Tria Giovan; (bottom) © Susan Teare, design: JMMDS

p. 187: © Allan Mandell, design: Wendy Pickin, Sidney, BC Mukilteo, WA

p. 188: (top) Brian Vanden Brink, design: South Mountain Company; (bottom) © Tria Giovan

p. 189: © Lee Anne White, design: Simmonds & Associates

p. 190: (left) © Randy O'Rourke, design: Nancy McCabe Garden Designs, Falls Village, CT; (top right) © Allan Mandell, design: Wendy Pickin, Sidney, BC; (bottom right)

© Mark Lohman, design: Sally Kanin Garden Design

p. 191: (top) © Tria Giovan; (bottom) © Tria Giovan

p. 192: (top) © Carolyn L. Bates Photography, design: Cynthia Knauf; (bottom) © Susan Teare, design: JMMDS

p. 193: © Bill Sumner Photography, design: JMMDS

p. 194: (left) © Ken Gutmaker, design: Lisa Port, APLD, Banyon Tree Design Studio; (right) © Susan Teare, design: JMMDS

p. 195: © Tria Giovan

p. 196: (top) © Susan Teare, design: JMMDS; (bottom) © Mark Lohman, design: Janet Lohman Design

p. 197: © Allan Mandell, design: Joan and Gary Cunningham, Victoria, BC

pp. 198–199: © Susan Teare, design: JMMDS

p. 200: (top) © Brian Vanden Brink, design: William Hanley, WMH Architects; (bottom) © Lee Anne White, design: Sean Weatherill, Weatherill & Associates

p. 201: © Susan Teare, design: George Zavis, Sight Design

pp. 202–203: © Janis Nicolay, design: Ron Rule Consultants Ltd.

p. 204: (top) © Susan Teare, design: JMMDS; (bottom) © Brian Vanden Brink, design: Dominic Paul Mercadante Architecture, Mohr & Seredin Landscape Architects

p. 205: (top) © Tria Giovan; (bottom left) © Susan Teare, design: John K Szczepaniak, Landscape Architect; (bottom right) © Susan Teare, design: JMMDS

p. 206: (left) © Lee Anne White, design: Simmonds & Associates; (top right) © Susan Teare, design: JMMDS; (bottom right) © Tria Giovan

p. 207: (top) © Randy O'Rourke, design: Nancy McCabe Garden Designs, Falls Village, CT; (bottom) © Tria Giovan

p. 208: (top) © Tria Giovan; (bottom) © Susan Teare, design: JMMDS

p. 209: © Tria Giovan

p. 210: (top) © Susan Teare, design: John K Szczepaniak, Landscape Architect; (bottom) © Susan Teare, design: MMDS

p. 211: (top) © Susan Teare, design:

John K Szczepaniak, Landscape Architect; (bottom) © Brian Vanden Brink, design: Dominic Paul Mercadante Architecture, Mohr & Seredin Landscape Architects

pp. 212–213: © Susan Teare, design: George Zavis, Sight Design

INDEX